T5-CRC-616

TWENTY-FIRST-CENTURY WORLD POWERS AND CHANGING ALIGNMENTS

University Press of America,® Inc.
Lanham · Boulder · New York · Toronto · Plymouth, UK

Copyright © 2012 by
University Press of America,® Inc.
4501 Forbes Boulevard
Suite 200
Lanham, Maryland 20706
UPA Acquisitions Department (301) 459-3366

Estover Road
Plymouth PL6 7PY
United Kingdom

Library of Congress Control Number: 2011940499
ISBN: 978-0-7618-5714-3 (paperback : alk. paper)
eISBN: 978-0-7618-5715-0

Dedication

To my wife Rekha who encouraged me throughout. Nishi my daughter and my son Avinash inspired me to write about our changing world.

Acknowledgements

I want to express my special thanks to my Editor Lindsay Macdonald who helped in giving the final version of the book. I also want to thank Victoria Koulakjian, Brij Raizada, Manu Bhatia and Bhagwan Dashairya for their valuable suggestions.I want to thank my publisher University Press of America for their support.

CONTENTS

Preface

When we open the entrance door of the twenty-first century, we see United States of America, Russia, China, India, England, France, Japan and Germany directing the highways of our universe, the planet Earth. The new comers are China and India and it seems they are going to play major roles in remolding our world. They are sitting in the front lane.

Next to the front lane are the countries which would have important roles to play. They are Brazil, South Korea and Italy.

There are countries which could derail the progress of the world. They can create problems and headache. They are: Afghanistan, Pakistan, Iran, Iraq and North Korea.

The rich countries of Europe will keep up their regular pace of life. The Eastern Europe would move forward slowly towards prosperity and growth.

Africa will take a long time to move into twenty-first century. Some of the Latin American countries would make good progress-like Argentina, Chile and Venezuela; however, most of the smaller countries would be beset with continuous non progression.

Globalization is good when the pace of progress is evenly spread; otherwise it does not bring about real change in global structure.

Technology and closer connectivity within nations would play a very important role in the twenty-first century.

The overwhelming scary feelings of nuclear holocaust would prevent the national leaders of the world to start a major conflict. In the near future, we do not see any dark clouds of World War III.

Global poverty, hunger, unemployment, destitution, illiteracy and ill health would not disappear soon from our world. By the end of the twenty-first century-we hope-things would be much better compared to what we have today. It is difficult to say that the world would sail smoothly, with out minor clashes and disruptions. With more prosperity spread out, there would be a bigger demand for arms and no substantial reduction in nuclear stockpiles. This situation may never change.

CHAPTER 1

Introduction

Cool and cozy relations between countries play a very significant and dominant role in establishing peace and prosperity in our world. The 21st century is seeing new countries embracing the challenges of leading and molding the shape and directions of our planet. The twentieth century superpowers – the United States and the USSR - are now being challenged by new emerging countries, notably China and India. In the post World War II world, England and France have taken backseat positions in the global political arena. Japan and Germany no longer command the military superiority they once enjoyed, though they exert tremendous influence in economic and financial sector. The United States has emerged as the only superpower and it is standing tall at the crossroads of globalization. There is no doubt that world politics is changing. Which will be the number one or number two, the most powerful country in the world? Only time will show with any certainty. However, there are visible signs that indicate there may not be any surprises

RATIONALE FOR ALIGNMENTS

Practical consideration of the historical connections as well as future needs dictate countries to link themselves with others. Most of the time, it is an evolutionary process; policies are not laid out in a hurry; they evolve over time. Religion, culture, race and historical connections- just a few of the many aspects of human behavior- play their role in establishing bilateral as well as international relations. Sometime, the political considerations become the most important factor in deciding with whom to connect with.

The history of mankind has evolved over several centuries; in this 21st century we have witnessed these evolutionary trends and transformations changing with high speed. Technology is opening new doors and new directions to take; bringing with it a new wave of thinking about ourselves. Many a times, we raise questions about our past and our future destination. Where are we precisely, and where we heading? Remember, human beings have always lived in groups. They have cultivated our languages, our cultures, our religions, indeed, our very ways of life, while living in groups. This process has been going on for a long time. Interactions that emerged between these different groups have set the foundation of our modern world.

The basic foundations-religion, language, culture, cordial or hostile relations for one another, history of alliance or war, future needs for mutual survival and prosperity have played vital roles in the past and it appears that they will play a greater role in the future, despite the fact that the world is getting smaller and more cohesive than ever before. These basic identifiers will play major roles in shaping the directions that the different countries of the world will move in, individually and as groups. Survival and mutual prosperity is the major consideration for forming groups. Next in line- language, culture, religion, common history and common views- take on important roles when we are considering bilateral or international relations.

Keeping in mind the above mentioned criteria for forming groups, let us consider some countries of Europe. England, Germany, France and Italy-all of them- have a common religion and that is Christianity. England and France were allies in World War II. All of these four countries have their own languages and have very rich cultural heritages individually. There exist some elements of common thinking and there are some points of disagreements between them. All of these countries are successful democracies; rich and prosperous. There are no animosities or clashes among these countries at present. All are members of NATO and European Union. We can figure out that these countries would be friendly since there is no real conflict of interest between these nations.

FOUNDATION FOR FORGING FUTURE ALLIANCES

Consider some countries of Asia. Look at their interactions, historical meeting grounds, religion, race, social and cultural affinities. Pacific Asia is dominated by Japan and China, whereas India is the dominant country of South Asia. Buddhism, Hinduism and Christianity play important part in the lives of a common man in these countries. History tells us that there were some regular interactions between Chinese and Indians till 1000 A.D. There was a continuous flow of religious thoughts between India and Japan. There were no adverse relations between these countries and its people. With no history of animosity against Japan and no adverse relations between the people, Japan and India could forge friendly relations. China and India could share a similarly cordial relationship, but this could go in wrong direction because of the mistrust that exists between the two countries. It will depend upon the leadership of these two countries to determine how they want to mold their relations. Global politics will have an important say in this matter. Broadly speaking, India, China, Japan and Korea will become good business partners as time moves on. However, trade and business is one thing while fraternity and close relationship is another thing. Korea, as an example, is in a very good position to establish excellent business relations with India because it does not have any negativity towards India.

The present global political scenario indicates that Japan and Korea would be good business partner as well as reliable friend of the United States. This might not be said for China and India. Down the road, India might become a good ally of the United States but China may attempt to stand on its own as a sole mega power. Russia and China may continue their friendly relations and progress towards a much stronger relationship; this seems to be a good possibility.

Consider India and England. After two hundred years of British rule and with a history of the past animosities, England and India have come out as close partners. There are two million Indians living in England. Indians enjoy success in the British social, political and business circles. The richest person in England happens to be an Indian. Indian business companies have made London as their base for doing business in Europe. Over these two centuries, British and Indians have taken from each other many aspects of daily living-social, cultural, and business practices. These are the basic elements in forging friendly and lasting alliances.

The most important aspect of all this is that these two countries want to establish closer relations between them. England and India have laid out strong foundations for enduring long-term friendly relations in terms of global alignments.

We firmly believe that India and England will move forward and progress in their cohesive relationship on the world stage. There are many common factors amongst these two countries that seem to indicate a close relationship. In Europe, Indians feel more at home in England than any other country. The major factor for this has been and is the millions of interactions on a daily basis between local Indians and the British people. Indians have assimilated many of the British ways of living. Most noticeably, they have done very well in education, trade and business establishments. Majority of European countries are engaged primarily with other European countries rather than with Asian nations.

Common language and cultural assimilation, along with similar technical meeting grounds solidify global relations. These links are fortified when we look at the relations between India and the United States. Whereas the United States has lost its glorious position as one of the most admired countries of the world in many parts of the world, it has retained this position in India. It has a very positive image with the majority of Indians. The Indian community in the United States has blended very well with the local traditions and its way of life. These fundamentals form the core of lasting, friendly relationships.

WORLD POWERS AND SUPER POWERS

World War II heralded United States of America as one of the greatest military powers. The United Soviet Socialist Republic (U.S.S.R) emerged also, as one of the most powerful military nations. These two countries had the privilege of being termed superpowers. No other country could match their military capabilities. Economically, the United States was far ahead of Soviet Russia. As time moved on, the Russian Economy went into tailspin in the early 1990's. The communist regime of the old USSR had fallen and Russia had changed to a semi-capitalistic society by this time. In 1989, when the USSR broke apart, the Russian economy was at the same level as any other emerging countries of the world in terms of economic structure. Considering all aspects, the United States has emerged as the only superpower today.

National wealth and military capabilities are the two most important assets that have to be considered when we judge the supremacy of any country. Looking from all wide angles, the United States is the world leader. The world is uni polar – no other country can exert as much influence in terms of wealth and military superiority as the United States can. Yet, there are other countries emerging rapidly to challenge the supremacy of the United States. China, India, Russia and Brazil are serious competitors to U.S.A.'s position. Individually and jointly, countries like England, France, Germany and Japan have the capabilities to become superpowers.

The last sixty years (1945-2005) have shown that the United States had the solid support of England in most of the major global issues. Russia, on the other hand, has been trying to show that the world is politically bipolar by trying continually to assert itself in global affairs. After communism failed in Russia, many of the so called Socialist nations - like India, Indonesia, Ceylon (Sri Lanka)-started moving towards the capitalistic structure of government. This change occurred because national income and the gross national product (GNP) are vital considerations along with military capabilities when we look at countries. From this perspective, it is no small wonder that Russia has lost its dominant position as a global leader. England and France, as well as Germany and Japan, are far ahead when we consider the national economy of Russia.

It seems that it will be very difficult to replace the United States as the most powerful country in the world. Japan and China, the second and third largest economies respectively, are far behind. Ten years from now, China's economy and military capabilities could challenge the United States with confidence.

It must be said that China has done a wonderful job in transforming itself from a poor agrarian country to a giant industrial manufacturing center. India is following the Chinese footsteps but still remains far behind China. Real competition could also emerge from the European Union in the future, but right now the EU is not cohesive enough to challenge American power.

We can place the countries of the world into two categories namely: Superpowers and World Powers. While it has been established that the Superpower title belongs to the United States for now, however, we might define a growing number of World Powers. We categorize World Powers as those countries where there are abundant opportunities to transcend class barriers, where stability and safety guarantee (to some extent) a life of one's own choosing, where freedom of expression is common, where democracy thrives, where there is justice for all its citizens, and where the future is taking shape for all of mankind. In addition, these countries should be relatively powerful in terms of military strength as well as in monetary resources.

World Powers have to be judged by these three major attributes: financial strength, military superiority, and population statistics. Based on these criteria, we have no hesitation in selecting the United States as the contemporary global superpower, and Russia, China, India and Brazil as emerging World Powers. England and France are established World Powers. Japan and Germany are financial powers. In this work, we shall discuss each of these countries: where they stand at present and where, we feel, they are heading in future. These countries are dictating the direction of world history. Nothing can be said to be absolute; however, trends and emerging scenarios in these countries serve as a good indicator as how things are moving, whether it is in the right direction or in reverse. With the United States established as the global superpower, this work will question what are the roles, characteristics, and capabilities of the other global players.

IS RUSSIA A SUPERPOWER

While they may have fallen from their role as a true global superpower, Russia is still a superpower when it comes to military strength. Along with the United States, Russia possesses the nuclear capability to destroy our planet ten times over. What happened in 1991 was the collapse of the USSR; its dissolution came due to a multitude of circumstances – both internal and external – forcing Russia to give up its control of Eastern European countries and central Asian republics which it had merged into the post-World War II conglomerate nation. Russia could not keep pace with the military build up of the United States. The primary reason was that they could no longer afford the enormous expenses of matching the United States growing military power. Simultaneously, Russian leaders began to realize the failings of Communism for their country. It was the death knell of Lenin. Thus the world changed in 1991; many countries of the world gave up on Communism and Socialism and started embracing the Capitalistic way of life.

Who has emerged from this drastic global change that took place in 1991? Russia has clearly declined from its Cold War state of power. It has begun to look like a fallen giant. Powers that will emerge in the wake of the USSR are China and India. England and France, both nuclear powers and of great military strengths, will not be able to continually compete with the growing powers of China and India in the future. While it is impossible to tell with any certainty when India and China will emerge as global superpowers, there are indications that they will do so some time in the immediate and foreseeable future. The reasons are clear: economic strength, large populations, sizeable military forces and inspired goals. While Japan and Germany similarly display some of these characteristics, present legal constraints limit their respective abilities to emerge as the powerful global forces that China and India seem on their way to achieving. At this time, China is leading aggressively economically and may take number two position pretty soon, surpassing Japan. China has taken number two position, now. Brazil has the potential to achieve similar benchmarks if it is provided with the right leadership and direction. As Russia becomes more sophisticated economically, it will move forward more rapidly towards prosperity like other Western European countries. Right now, it sill remains far behind. However, we should concentrate on Russia, China and India as the major power players following the United States.

In a decade or two, Russia may come on par with Chinese economy and at that juncture Russia and China might match up in terms of military and economic considerations. However, China has to catch up with Russia from the military point of view.

India does not seem to be gaining upon China in terms of either military strength or economic growth as it is run under a democratic system. Delays, corruption, lack of inspired leadership and non-focused plans might derail the Indian train. However, there remain reasons to believe that India will reach its desired global status, whether it is able to do so with the speed of China or with a slower pace; it has to be seen.

EMERGING WORLD POWERS

So who are the present winners and losers and who will eventually emerge in the long term? With the present geopolitical analysis, we feel that Russia will retain the Super power position in the world solely on the basis of its military superiority. China is a close runner up along with India; they make up the list of emerging dominant world powers.

Just as our life is a race, so is the case with every nation; we must decide how to run it. Consider India and China and their chance of taking the first runner up position. We all know China is a communist country with a strong dictatorship; there is no democracy, no freedom of expression, instead there is a sheer, solid rock society of ruthless, communist leaders. What we have seen about Mao or Stalin seems to be equally true with regards to the present Chinese leadership. Tiananmen Square in Beijing is a testimonial example. On the other side is India, a democratic country with full freedom of expression. Both of these countries have a long way to go to catch up with the advanced countries of the Western Europe in terms of standard of living. There remains substantial poverty in both countries. China and India are capable of achieving phenomenal economic progress; however, to eradicate poverty and raise the standard of living for the masses seems a long way off.

Despite these problems with poverty, India and China are progressing strongly in terms of economic growth. With this positive factor, both of these countries are trying to build a massive military force. China is leading India, from the economic as well as the military point of view. Thus, India must begin to catch up with China if it wishes to rival its growing power.

When we go back to history, we note that the Communist China had waged border wars with India, Russia and Vietnam. Beijing leaders keep up unleashing war propaganda against Taiwan, though their leaders strongly tell the world that China is a peace loving country. The close Chinese relationship with Russia serves as a double-edged sword against the United States power. If we think strategically, the United States would like to have India to counter this potential and growing threat. Will India go along with the United States in this capacity? It is difficult to say. Indian leaders discount this notion; they do not want to be in the shadows of the United States.

In 1962, China had inflicted a strong defeat to India. At this time, India does not have the moral and military courage to tell China that Tibet is not a province of greater China. A stronger Indian military force can make the difference. India can advance the freedom cause of the Tibetan people. It could allow the Indian leaders to take on the cause of Tibet in a way which it is unable to push, under the present conditions. The Indian leadership has to think that it is the United States alone that is capable of telling China that Tibet is not a province of their nation. Indian leadership must understand that it is the United States alone that could help India, in the event of aggression by China. Russia might mediate or remain neutral under these conditions. It is doubtful if it supports India; Russia as a former communist country has political leanings towards China. Since India and China lag far behind U.S.A and Russia in terms of military resources, both of these countries would not dare to confront the mighty forces of the United States and Russia. For another decade or so, India and China would avoid open clash or aggression against each other, because the United States is there to intervene. While Russia is trying to build a more sophisticated modern military force that is certainly far ahead of the Chinese capabilities; however, it seems likely that China will continue to exceed Russia economically. India too possesses the ability to exceed traditional World powers. Yet, if the political picture in India continually gets mired up in corruption and produces unstable governments then , there is no doubt that China would become the next world superpower.

It is the nature of democracy which dictates the good aspects coupled with negative factors that India is going through. China will continue to be rigid, stable and focused; factors that could make it go farther than India in terms of global power and influence. It is up to Indian leadership to decide what it wants and how it is going to achieve it. It can move faster than China in its quest to become a superpower if there is a determination and the proper environment to make it happen.

Still, the nature of global politics is unpredictable. Back in early Eighties, China was still a poor developing country. India was not even in the growth mode till the early Nineties. Russia saw the USSR disintegrate in 1991. Observing these countries in 2008, it demonstrates a stark contrast. Beijing hosted the most dazzling Olympics ever recorded in the history. India's gross domestic product (GDP) is growing by nine percent. Russia is flushing with billions of petro dollars and once again acting as military power to be reckoned with. The last two decades have greatly changed the traditional powers and produced new and growing powers. How China, India and Russia are going to interact with each other is a political guess work. As these countries move along their respective paths, the world will be watching with interest how they are going to influence the rest of the world.

EMERGING POWERS: INDIA AND CHINA

China has a big lead over India in terms of economic and military strengths. With 1.3 billion Chinese and 1.1 billion Indians and fifty percent of people living in rural areas in each country respectively, the population logistics appear to be evenly matched. The biggest difference is the political systems: democracy in India versus authoritarian rule in China. Though China is a communist country, it still exists as one of the most favorable zones for business with emerging capitalistic practices. It has lifted millions of people from poverty. Lot of credit should be given to the Chinese government for making this happen in essentially thirty years. By sheer hard work and good business practices, China has become an economic powerhouse to be reckoned with.

With all this steep progress in industrialization, China does not have many fundamental rights, like freedom of speech, political and religious freedoms, and many of the other social norms and behaviors found in democratic nations. It has established a solid base for future growth and expansion in terms of economic growth, but it will need to address its own issues with basic questions of human rights. The present leadership stresses that it will come gradually, something that only time can truly tell. As the middle class becomes a larger proportion of Chinese society, there are bound to be more freedoms available to the common man and woman of China.

When we compare India with China in terms of individual freedoms it is like we are comparing entirely different worlds. You can speak freely, believe freely, and live freely in India. This is a tremendous step in addressing issues of human rights and freedoms, something that China has to learn this from its neighbor.

ADDRESSING POTENTIAL CONFLICTS

With the potential for conflict omnipresent during these periods of accelerated growth in India and China, it must be speculated what would happen should these nations decide to unleash a major war over disputed territories or over the sovereignty of Tibet? During 1962, when China and India found themselves in a similar engagement, the United States helped India by providing military supplies and armaments. Today, there are only two countries, the United States and Russia, who could sway the direction of such a military conflict. Analyzing another scenario, the United States would like to maintain friendly relations and support of India, in the event of any eventual dispute between the U.S. and China.

Does this mean that India should align itself with the United States? It is an argument with some great merits. What must be asked is whether or not, it is in India's best interest to move into this relationship with the United States and ignore the growing power of China. There exists some potential that China and Russia may join hands against India, though it is equally likely that Russia might maintain a neutral position between India and China. The United States appears hesitant to go against China unless it has very strong grounds to do so. It is also true that the Chinese will not, in the immediate future, venture to take action against the United States.

After 1962 India-China war, probability dictated that India and the United States would like to link their countries closer for more security. Sill, as things stand today, India and China could again become friendly given the right policies. However, such relations are not part of the foreseeable future. It is true that India and China would both be losers if they chose to ignore each other. Given the benefits that exist, would they be able to carve out their relations on friendly and mutually beneficial foundations?

Logistics and historical cultural relations between India and China can not be ignored. Strong strategic relations between China and Pakistan have become an irritant factor as far as Indian-Chinese relations are concerned. The relations between China and Pakistan are based purely on an anti-India platform; both of these countries have gone to war against India and therefore stand to benefit from supporting one another. India and Pakistan, both nuclear powers, have common cultures, yet are against each other partly due to religious differences. These three nations could, in the long run, enjoy friendly relations, though suspicions dictate that mistrust might continue for sometime. Nobody can predict all the ramifications of changing times. Would India and China develop a sustainable relationship? We can conclude with some confidence that India and China would embark on a mutual road to prosperity rather than go to war.

INDIA AND RUSSIA

Back in sixties and seventies, Russia and India were close. India was following the socialist policies and the leaders of both countries were good friends. Things started changing in the eighties and the nineties saw the relationship take a different direction. Russian leaders were not as enthusiastic in maintaining the exclusive relations with India that had existed in the sixties. In the past, Russia had supported India, notably in its dispute of Kashmir accession to Pakistan, whereas the United States often favored Pakistani interests.

Furthermore, in 1991, India moved towards the free-market economy while Russia too, went through similar changes, with the disintegration of the USSR.

Beginning in the nineties and further on, India began to gravitate towards the United States and move away from its close relationship with Russia. By this time, about two million Indians had settled down in the United States and they were assimilating into the mainstream with good success. This close interaction with the United States became the defining factor in establishing healthy and friendly relations that had never truly existed before between these two nations. Language, mutual respect and emerging business dealings, especially in information technology, were the important factors in the mapping of this closer relationship between India and the United States. The present rising stature of India owes its debt to its own information technology reservoir.

Even today, India and Russia do not have any major I.T related business dealings, whereas more than sixty percent of India's software business is linked with the United States. As present conditions exist, India and Russia would be good business partners; India has in the past, purchased most of its military hardware-fighters, aircraft carrier, tanks and other armaments from Russia. This trend may continue in the near future too. So the business side between India and Russia seems like that it will be maintained and thus there is a strong probability that other aspects of cordial and friendly relations may make further inroads. Still, it seems this will take some time unless some drastic change comes along. Russia seems primarily interested in exercising its influence over its own commonwealth countries rather than spending too much time fostering relations with India.

However, Russia will continue to have closer relations with China as their history with communism has created sustainable bonds. In a scenario where India and China enter armed conflict, chances are that Russia would like to take a neutral position and only as a last resort side with their Chinese friends. Russia is much ahead in terms of military capabilities when compared to China and India. Both of these countries are customers of Russian military equipment and technology.

Russia would like to take a balanced posture when it comes to China and India, as both countries are potential Superpowers and deserve serious attention. The present Russian position regarding India's relations with the United States is "as long as India does not go drastically opposite to the Russian interests, it is O.K." Russia understands the military needs of India and India can not ignore what Russia could offer. It is a mutually inclusive sphere.

RUSSIA AND CHINA

As mentioned before, Russia and the United States were the only two superpowers after World War II and now, at present, this coveted designation belongs only to the United States. Russia is designated as a regional superpower. China is emerging not only as a regional power it is a rising, up coming superpower. Russia is a superpower if we consider only its military; economically it is far behind the western European countries. China is trying to increase its military power. Most of its military shopping is done through Russia. Back in the sixties, there was a border dispute between Russia and China, but this didn't amount to anything substantial. Since then, Russia and China have enjoyed a cordial and healthy relationship. Still, there is room for potential conflict to emerge in the uncertainty of the future.

When we look at international relations, these two countries react in a similar fashion. Both of these countries have mutually exclusive area of influence; there is no clash there. When we analyze the common links between these countries, there are some important meeting grounds. The most influential factor is a shared history of communism and authoritarian rule. China knows that it can not overtake Russia in terms of military power in the immediate future. Yet Russia knows it well that China is a big country with a huge population; it has the military capability to defend itself very well.

With this background, we can say with some assuredness that these two countries may never fight a war against each other. Questions become more meddled when one wonders what would happen if there were a dispute between Russia and the United States or if there is a war between India and China- what would be the immediate reaction under these conditions-these are tough questions to answer. Under the present global political environment, the chances of happening any of these scenarios are very dim. The most probable answer that we think of is that it would start a World War. Countries like China, India, Russia and the United States can not afford to go to war. The world can not afford this confrontation. The people of the world understand very well what it means when nuclear powers go in the wrong directions.

When we say that the United States and England will swim in the same boat, that saying is true for the Chinese and Russian relationship. Furthermore, each country would respect the sphere of influence that the other country holds. For example, China would not become involved in central Asia where Russia has historical relations. Same way Russia will not interfere in South East Asia where China has established close relations with its neighboring countries. In the event of conflict or dispute, would Russia and China ally against Japan or India? It is most likely not going to happen. China has to do lot of catching up from a military standpoint and would not engage in action against other countries unless some radical situation arises. The same argument holds true in the case of Russia too. If China goes to war against Taiwan, the United States would side with Taiwan while Russia would be more hesitant, at least in the initial stages, to go against Taiwan.. In the Pacific and Southeast Asia, there are three regional superpowers - India, China and Russia –they will play important roles on the world political stage. In other words, the joint partnership of China and Russia could prove to be very beneficial to our world. Consider the case of North Korea, China and Russia could help the western countries to stop the nuclear program of North Koreans. Russia and China have strong relations with the Communist North Korea.

RUSSIA-THE EMERGING SUPERPOWER

Before 1991, Russia dominated the world events along with the United States. Things have since changed and Russia is now considered an emerging world power, primarily due to its lack of economical clout. Militarily, it is still the second most powerful country after the U.S. When the USSR disintegrated, it lost the global political power and prestige that it had enjoyed in the seventies and eighties. During previous times, Russia had tremendous influence with the governments of China, India, Egypt, Eastern Europe, Latin American countries and many countries on the African continent. The effects of the fall of the USSR were similar to, when England lost its glory after World War II. The economical crunch was the deciding point for the decline of these nations.

Russia embraced communism in 1917 and, after almost seven decades, it could not transform itself into a prosperous, wealthy country despite many strides of continuous progress, notably in the field of nuclear and space technology. Many of the Asian countries-India, China and Egypt – adopted the Russian model of governance during this time period. The Russian leaders were welcomed guests in many countries, unlike the Americans who were associated with British Imperialism. From this time, evident change has taken place. In 2010, Russia has few close friends and it no longer commands the same respect and prestige that it enjoyed during the Cold War years.

The demise of the communism took away the sheen, glamour, and mystic of Russian socialism. China, although a communist nation politically, is perhaps the most capitalistic society in the world as far as business matters are concerned. China is now emerging as one of the most influential countries in the world mainly because of this economic strength. Russia is now far behind China with regards to economic achievement and Gross Domestic production.

Russia still has good political relations with countries like China, many central Asian countries, North Korea, the Middle Eastern countries of Iran, Syria, Palestine, and Egypt, Vietnam, India, Venezuela and many more. However, it does not carry a globally dictating voice. The Russian sphere of influence has greatly diminished in Asia. China is perhaps the most enduring ally of Russia at this point in time. If anything dramatic arises, some unpredictable event in the realm of global politics, Russia and China will join hands together. India might not. Israel is not pro-Russia; Syria, Palestine and Iran have no influencing power in the world political stage despite their relations with Russia.

The present leadership of Russia realizes that it is in its own interest to be on friendly terms with America and Western nations in order to help improve its standard of living. It can not afford to antagonize the West; it has to learn a lot from the West if it wants to replace communism with democratic governance. It is not an easy task and will take sometime before their country would be flourishing in all aspects again.

The world will consist of many powerful countries and Russia will continue to be one of them. No one country will dominate the events of the world progress. The nuclear powers – the United States, Russia, England, France, China, India and Pakistan - will be those countries whose voice will continue to enjoy greater influence on the global stage. North Korea, Iran and Israel cannot be counted out. If we are looking for a peaceful, prosperous planet, vigilance must be maintained to prevent the arrogance of leaders from deteriorating and breaking the growing global connections, possibly with another world war.

PRESENT SCENARIOS AND FUTURE PROJECTIONS

The global race for power is taking new turns. Who will be number one and who will keep progressing towards new heights? The answer is not difficult. As things stand today and probably will be-for at least the next decade- the world's leading most country is the United States. Economically, militarily, socially, it remains the country that leads the rest of the world. Today, the United States exists as the world's sole true superpower, a title that it will more than likely enjoy for several more decades. There was a time when Russia too met these qualifications, but it has since faltered. Still, there is no doubt that Russia is the second most powerful country as far as military strength is concerned. However, the nation falls short when it comes to other deciding factors, such as those of national income, gross national product, democratic institutions, and social mobility amongst others.

Which other countries have emerged and entered in this race for world power? It is not difficult to find the true leaders in these groups. We know how fast the emerging countries like China and India are challenging the old powers of Western Europe At the end of World War II, Japan and Germany lost their prestige. They cannot be considered, under present legal standing, as great military powers. We can safely count them out of the race for supremacy unless powerful global circumstances change the whole scenario. So the leading contenders to challenge the United States' stature as world leader are China and India.

We have seen and will continue to explore how these countries stack up with regards to numerous factors, such as population demographics, current political institutions, class mobility, economic and military powers, etc. China and India have huge population-more than one billion each. At present, their economies are growing rapidly. China's gross domestic product will cross five trillion dollars and become the second largest economy worldwide. India is moving along at a good rate economically as well, with hopes that it will replace all the Western countries in terms of GDP.

However, nothing can be taken for granted and these unpredictable questions have to be looked into thoroughly. There are many interesting scenarios that come into the geopolitical power game. During the Cold War between the USSR and the United States, China was a non-contender to these two powers. Presently, China is taking some bold moves to confront the supremacy of the United States. Still, it is clear that China does not match up against the United States in terms of military strength. But what happens if China and Russia collude against the United States? Is there any possibility of such a scenario? Would there be another clash between India and China, as it had happened in 1962? Does the United States want India to stand against China? Will Russia be a most favored nation for India? Will China become the second superpower? These and other related questions have to be examined very carefully and with all the necessary inquisitive probing. We are taking for granted that the United States will remain the sole superpower at least for another decade or so. However, things might change very fast in this race of world supremacy, as demonstrated by the changes that have taken place in recent years. Still, there is no doubt China is the leading challenger in this game of world supremacy.

CHAPTER 2

United States of America

WEALTH: THE FINANCIAL POWER

The United States is the richest country in the world. Per capita income is around fifty thousand dollars. The federal government budget runs into trillions. It is a country where millionaires do not make any headlines. It is a country full of natural resources as well as man made resources. Innovation and new product development has become a natural trait. People are not afraid to work hard; this attribute and their highly entrepreneurial nature have made the country a great nation. A country is rich when its people have talents, possess technical and business knowhow, and have a desire to succeed. The government encourages this spirit of personal freedom. People are not looking for employment all the time. Many may want to create jobs for them and others instead. By achieving the American Dream, a person feels that he has achieved something big in terms of material wealth, as well as the other ideals associated with it. Most of the time, talented people are rewarded accordingly. Dreaming big is the mantra of the nation. If you have the determination and courage, you can fulfill your dreams in America.

MILITARY STRENGTH

The greatest military power in the world is the United States of America. These days, it is the nuclear arsenal that carries with it the most importance; other forces are of a secondary consideration. Along with Russia, these two countries can destroy the entire planet many times if they decide to use their nuclear weapons supply. Other nuclear powers are England, France, China, India, Israel and Pakistan. Weapons of mass destruction (WMD) can become a source of great danger to the world if they fall into the hands of overzealous religious fanatics. At the same time, military strength is a powerful tool to make things happen in the world. Countries like China and India want to increase their military strength so that their policies and declarations will carry with them greater respect and authority worldwide. In today's world, when countries like the United States, Russia, England and France say something, others listen. This will become true with China and India too, sometime in the near future, should they continue to build up their military forces.

There was a time when morality and ethics reigned supreme in global politics, if only for a short span of time, but this has since waned. The people and the nations are tuned into military considerations more than at any other time. Political leaders consider the military weapon the ultimate weapon in their dealings with other nations. It is therefore very important to look at the military strength of countries who want to be classified as world powers or superpowers. Nuclear technology has changed the world. Countries that have nuclear bombs and missiles could threaten other countries who do not have these armaments with more authority and power. The leaders of these countries have a tremendous responsibility to use their judgment properly in times of adversity and dire necessity. The use of these weapons would bring the end of peace and prosperity to an affected region for a long time to come. Japan had seen it. Humanity does not want to repeat this holocaust.

POPULATION DEMOGRAPHICS

Population statistics are very significant in today's world when we analyze the world powers. Countries like China and India, with populations exceeding more than a billion respectively, have a tremendous effect on world economics, whether it is through trade, social ramifications, innovation, new ways of doing things, or through new ways of thinking. The affect of the population is tangential and exponential. A country with a high standard of living but with a small population and consequently with a small army cannot be included on a list of world powers and potential superpowers. It does not have enough military clout to influence other countries. This notion carries over into the realm of global politics. Many Western European countries have established themselves with a high standard of living but they do not have nuclear technology nor do they have large standing armies. These countries do have some leverage, but they do not have the military superiority to survive any sustained conflict. The qualifications to be included on the world powers list includes: the wealth of the nation; military superiority and population pyramid. The United States of America, with a population of more than three hundred millions people, with the largest military force, and as the richest country in the world thus has the biggest impact on contemporary world politics.

Russia, with the second largest military power, about one hundred fifty millions people and being not a wealthy country in terms of gross national income does not carry a similar influence due to its economic standing. It will take a long time before ordinary Russian people can boast about their standard of living. We have included Russia on our list because it seems very likely that Russian standard of living will improve over time, perhaps even very shortly during these days when oil and natural gas prices are rising. There is also the likelihood that their population will increase. When all three attributes are met squarely by Russia, it can then challenge the United States' position very strongly.

It is said that it is the quality of people that matters and not the quantity. This is both partially correct and partially incorrect. We have seen in the Korean War where the might of American army was on full display yet it could not vanquish the huge force of the Chinese army. Numbers matter. During the

World War II, it was the superiority in the numbers of the Allied forces that eventually led to the downfall of the German war machine.

FUTURE SCENARIOS:
THE UNITED STATES TEN YEARS FROM TODAY

Wealth and Prosperity

As we look towards the future, projecting into the next decade, we predict that United States of America will still be the richest country in the world as it is today. We do not see any other country on the horizon that is capable of taking this top economic position. There are other countries that will be gaining quickly on the United States in terms of economic growth, but we do not see any nation capable of replacing the United States for a long period of time. There are number of reasons to think along these lines. The first factor is entrepreneurship, as the people are sold on individual enterprise system. They have seen how it could change one's life. Private enterprise thrives in the country and the people excel at it. The existing wealth of the country would not dissipate unless many major mistakes are made by the government. The second reason for retaining the title is the nation's business environment. Government rules and regulations and the strength of the financial institutions secure a healthy marketplace. These are in place right now, and we do not see anything major that would lead us to predict a drastic change. As long as political leaders are more or less uncorrupted in terms of money, bribery, etc., the country will continue to move forward in creating more wealth than it ever has in the past. The gross national income of the common man and woman would go up from its present levels. More of the minority group members will be able to join the middle and high middle class status during this time frame. No doubt, the rich will become richer in the coming decade.

Similarly, we see many European countries moving up the economic ladder. China and India will also be in this economic fast lane, along with Japan, Korea, Russia and Brazil.

Military Strength

We have concluded without any reservation that the United States currently holds supremacy from the military perspective. However, Russia is a big challenger. Still, these positions might not change. Though China and India both have growing military strength, it seems unlikely that Russia would let its military strength dip into the third position. The present stockpile of nuclear arsenal of United States and Russia is huge and it would be a difficult task for any other country to surpass these supplies. France and England will continue to increase their military strength but will still be far behind. During this next decade, it is therefore not unlikely that China and India will move to the third and fourth positions in terms of military capability and strength.

Nuclear weapons are not the only factor moving forward; conventional weapons are changing war with advancements in technology. Sophisticated, automatic, and robotic fighting tools are changing the ways war is fought. It is going to take a more important place in planning and staging a war in the near future. Nuclear intercontinental missiles and other futuristic weapons will play important part in future wars. This will undoubtedly benefit those countries that will be advanced in technical knowhow and rich enough to carry out further research work. The United States of America has this capability now and it seems it will continue to hold this position for the next decade and beyond.

Population Factor: Demographics

Ten years from now, the United States of America will have a larger population than it is today, perhaps around 330 millions or more .The positive effect of having this larger population is that the wealth of the country will continue to take a bigger share. In other words, the economy and population will be in sync and continue to grow together. We know how a growing population could pull down a country if the overall wealth of the country does not go up. Fortunately, the United States will grow in population as well as generate more wealth than it has now. This is how we see the future for the United States of America.

We can also see that the minority communities, mainly the Latino community, African Americans, and Asian immigrants, growing much faster than the Caucasian community. This is mainly because of the differences in the birth rates and family preferences. However, the white population will still be the majority for the next twenty years or so.

A hundred percent meltdown of cultural differences may not be possible. However, different sections of the society would be moving towards more cohesion and common mixing. The main reason for this is that the country is focused more upon achieving monetary gains than any other commodity. As long as the common person is able to go up in life and achieve his/ her goals and dreams, the country will continue to progress into the future with success.

Ten years from now, India may become the most populated country in the world and surpass China. The population explosion in these countries have many disadvantages because both nations are still far behind in terms of total wealth causing there to exist a lingering poverty that will not disappear in a short period of time. These two emerging countries will take a couple of decades to reach a standard of living which already exists in Western Europe, Japan, Canada and Australia. Large populations in China and India will continue to slow the national economies of these countries and socio-political tensions could become a great threat to the advancement of both nations. The situation in the United States is different. It is the richest country in the world and it is highly industrialized. It can absorb more population without losing its position as the world's shining star.

U.S.A AND OTHER INFLUENTIAL COUNTRIES OF THE WORLD

We have to analyze and dissect the relationship among the world powers. These links are founded on many grounds and fundamentals. Culture, religion, race, language, location, history, needs, and many other factors play the decisive role in creating these bonds and links. These factors could change as the needs of the nations change. The games in the world politics are played with no fixed rules and regulations; they are bended as situation warrants. Two close allies of today may or may not be close allies of tomorrow. The behavior of political leadership is always subject to change. Leaders of the country could change the course of history if they desire to do so. Poor countries of years gone by, are emerging fast to become the leaders of today. The established leaders of today's world are looking for new friends and allies. We shall look into these relationships, country by country.

The United States and the United Kingdom

These two countries have put up a solid front and have supported each other in most of the foreign policy matters, notably in Iraq, Iran, North Korea and Afghanistan. It has been a strong global alliance. Former Prime Minister Tony Blair was a good friend of former President Bill Clinton, and was a good ally of President George W. Bush. It has been observed that the personal relationship between leaders has a strong influence in forming such alignments. Historically, this relationship goes back to World War II; the United States supported England in its difficult times and it seems like, the United Kingdom considers it a moral duty to support United States when it needs the most. England was the most powerful nation in the world a few decades ago and stretching further back into the past. The relations between these two countries have been friendly and smooth. We do not see any major rift or dividing alliance between these two countries in the near future.

Let us also look at how things will stand ten years from today. Historically, these two countries have stood with each other throughout most of their collective histories. They share many things in common, but their global role is one of the most common denominators. At one point in time, England ruled over the world, something that is no longer the case. However, it still commands a dominant position within such groups as the United Nations, and on the stage of global politics in general. Since the United States is now the only superpower in the world, it seems natural that these two countries should cooperate with one another. One of the most important aspects of this relationship is that there is no conflicting area of influence where there could be a potential clash. Both countries know and respect their global roles and responsibilities.

Whether there is a Conservative Party or Labor Party in power, the Prime Minister in England and a Republican or a Democratic President in the United States would get along just fine; the relations between the United States and

England will not change drastically. Personal relations between the U.S. President and the Prime Minister of England possess the power to either bring these countries closer or make them further apart.

Most of the people in the United States originally came from England; there exist lot of family, cultural, social, economic, and other bonds between the people. The present Queen of England is still popular in the United States. There is a genuine feeling of understanding between the people of England and that of United States when compared to the other nations of the world. Both of these countries have fought together in World Wars and very recently in Iraq and Afghanistan.

Can these countries continue to rely and count on one another? It seems the answer is yes unless there are radically different points of view between the top leaders of the two countries. Personalities will contribute to this relationship just like any other. Close friendship between President Clinton and Prime Minister Tony Blair is a true example of a solid relationship between the two nations. Thus, since World War II, England and the United States have garnished and maintained a new and robust relationship between their nations.

Future Relations between the United States and England

Democratic institutions are bound to have some disagreements, but this is natural. It is amazing to see that England and the United States have concurred with each other in almost all the major policies, whether it was related to NATO alliances or the Global Financial Crisis of 2009. Prime Minister Gordon Brown and President Obama formulated a common strategy to stop the global financial collapse and took the lead to move forward. There is so much understanding between the people and the governments of these two countries that it could be safely projected that the future relations between the United States and England would be friendly and very cooperative. Thus, it is our assessment that the next decade will see no drastic changes than the previous ten and they will continue their relationship.

The United States and Canada

The largest trading partner of the United States is Canada. Next to England, Canada is the most reliable U.S. partner. It must be understood that Canada is an equal partner. Therefore, it can chart its own course which may or may not coincide with U.S. interest. In the recent past, the relations have been overwhelmingly not friendly or very cordial. This is mostly because of personality differences between the top leaders of the two countries. Also, it is because Canada wants to show that it will follow its own independent policy.

Foreign policy, trade regulations, sociopolitical interpretations, and other aspects of every day life will not be a carbon copy of the United States. It will be Canadian in spirit and nature, distinct from the American frame, though the hues may be intermingled and exchanged comfortably. Canada has a population of around 30 million- compared to the U.S. populations of around 300 million –and is therefore not a military power nor does it have anywhere close to the military capability of the United States. However, it has a very high standard of living to accommodate its smaller population, on par with Australia and other Western European countries.

There are other distinct differences between the United States and Canada. Canada is a member of the Commonwealth Nations. Queen Elizabeth is the Head of the State and the Governor General of Canada is appointed by the Queen of England. Canada is a bi-lingual state with English and French as the two official languages of the country. Canada has nationally funded health insurance, meaning that every individual has health insurance paid for by the government.

The Central Bank of Canada has set up tight fiscal rules and regulations so that private banks cannot indulge in high risk transactions. This difference in the banking system of the United States and Canada saved the Canadians from the fiscal meltdown that decimated the economies of the United States and England. It might prove true that calculated risk taking is better than high risk taking in financial transactions. Not a single Canadian bank failed in the recent financial turmoil that brought about a world crisis. Canadians enjoy more social benefits from the government compared to American citizens.

Canada and the United States are the founding members of the North America Free Trade Association. This agreement has helped create these two countries as the largest trading partners in the world. The standard of living for Canadians is very high: gross national income per capita of Canada is around $43,000 whereas that of the United States is $50,000.

What shape will relations between Canada and the United States be in during this next decade? We can predict that they will continue to be friendly and close. There are no areas of major conflict between these two countries. There exists a lot of common ground between the two. The governing factor of closeness would be dictated by the personalities of the top leaders, the President of United States and the Prime Minister of Canada. Unlike Mexico, Canada will continue to be a close ally, especially without any border tensions or immigration problems.

Future Assessment

At the present moment the relations between the United States and Canada are excellent. Canadian troops are fighting along with the American soldiers in Afghanistan and there are no serious disputes. The foreign policy of Canada may or may not be same as that of the United States, but both countries understand each other needs and objectives in the global political arena very well. Countries like Canada and Australia could take global influential positions if they follow the immigration policies of the United States. A large, technically savvy and risk taking work force is needed to achieve such global status.

Canadians would not like to see the United States as a big brother, but would like to be treated as equal partners in every aspect of mutual respect.

The United States and Australia

The government of Australia headed by Prime Minister John Howard was cooperative and friendly with President George W. Bush. Unlike many European countries, the Australian Government supported American policies in Iraq. This support level may or may not be lasting; the future Australian Prime Minister may not adhere to American foreign policy in the same way or even at all. Australian foreign policies are subjected to its geographical location in the Pacific, with its close proximity to Asia. Its major trading partners are Japan, China and several other Asian countries. This creates the need for the Australian global alliances to be linked to its Asian neighbors. There are close ties to England, adopting the Queen of England as their Queen too. Security of the land is taken care of by United Kingdom and United States. Like Canada, Australia will most likely follow a strong friendly alliance with United States and England. The probability of the United States and Australia following divergent global policies is somewhat negligible. Though Australia is interlocked with Asian countries in trade, immigration, and safety matters, the foreign policies of Australia would not oppose the policies laid out by England and the United States. These countries have lot of common bonds through religion, culture, language, history, and similar global perspectives. Though Australia has a very high standard of living with a GNI at around $43,000, it is not a military power. The population is twenty two million people; this is no match to the growing populations of India and China. The chemistry of the top leaders of both Australia and the United States will play an important role in the next ten years. There may not be any major differences in the future of their relationship. Relations between these countries should continue to be close.

The United States and Russia

The Russian leader in 1991, Mr. Gorbachev, changed the history of the world. The Cold War between the United States and the USSR thawed, than melted away. It had a tremendous affect on many countries on the European, Asian and African continents. The two superpowers of that era fell apart and the U.S. emerged as the sole entity. President Reagan played a big role in this transformation. The two countries have tried to be friendly to each other from the end of the Cold war. However, long term relations between the two countries will be governed by many variables. Once the economic weakness of Russia changes its course, things might again be moving the world back towards a bipolar state. The Russian government will start exercising its overall strengths in relations with other countries, especially in the Middle East, Asia and Africa. With the European Union going strong in terms of stability, security, and overall prosperity, it looks like that Russian government will no longer meddle in European affairs, especially if it pits them against U.S. or British interests. Whether there will be a strong alliance between Russia and the United States is a matter of strong speculation and circumstances.

It appears the relations between United States and Russia will not be as cordial in the coming decade as they were during 1995-2005. The Russian economy is changing; the high prices of oil and natural gas have made a tremendous impact. The standard of living for the common man in Russia is much better than it was ten years ago. Though Russia is still far behind the Western countries in terms of economic wealth, it is still able to exude and utilize its military strength, using its nuclear arsenal as a leveraging tool. There can be no doubt that Russia is on par with the United States as far as its nuclear arsenal is concerned. President Putin has started playing the old Cold War games, once again talking about bipolar superpowers. He is not happy to see the United States as the only superpower. He wants a throwback to an era when there were two true superpowers. He is seeing Russia gain ground slowly and steadily. In the due course of time it could attain as good a position as any other Western country of today in terms of gross national income.

Russia has a population exceeding 140 million plus at present, and the chances are it will grow fast compared to the Western countries. It is an important consideration to look at. However, the chances are that the Russian leadership will not openly challenge the American power within the coming decade. Still, there is the probability that the next few decades might see the return of the old Cold War scenario, returning it to the forefront of global politics. Russian pride and nationalism could play a very important role in shaping the future policies of Russia towards United States and other Western countries.

Russia has seen it all: from a communist to a semi-capitalist country, from the position of a superpower to being relegated to a secondary world power. It has gone through some rough times in history. The present leaders of Russia know that economically Russia is still a poor country compared to the United States, and that this is unlikely to change in the near future. Russia's gas and oil is bound to put the country on a path of growing prosperity in the long run. However, the capitalistic Russia has to learn all the business techniques of their new society, just as China did, and than the country might begin to transform. The United States knows the military strength of Russia, especially its nuclear capabilities, and it can not afford to openly affront the rigid military positions of the Russian government. The thaw of the Cold War should be maintained by both countries in the interests of global peace and prosperity.

The United States and China

When examining the relations between China and U.S.A, we have to look into couple of important factors. These include the emergence of the Chinese economy as the second largest in the world, its boisterous population of 1.3

billion, its existence as a non-democratic, communist country, and a history of unpredictable behavior towards other countries. China has fought against the United States and its allies in the Korean War in 1950; it has occupied Tibet; it attacked India in 1962; it had a border war with Russia. Though the present leaders of China proclaim that China is a peace loving country, they are simultaneously spending large amounts of money building up their armaments, trying to create a superior military force. With this background, there can be no wonder as to why Former President Bush feels that it is important to have India allied with the United States as a counter force to balance the region. Japan has cast its full support with the United States with regards to global political policies. Still, it is the fact that it is the third largest economy in the world, but without military power. Thus, American policy has to find some other viable sources and alignments to counterbalance the growing Chinese global threat.

The Great Leap of China and the U.S Policies

China has done a wonderful job in raising the standard of living for millions of its people. It is a shining example to other developing nations of the world. A communist country becoming a great capitalist society has shown unbelievable success. With a population of 1.3 billions accompanied by growing military build up, China could be a possible threat to the United States' power and prestige. If China and Russia ally against the United States, it will be a big problem. The world will be thrown into old threats and counter-threats from these nations; struggle for power would start new cycle in world politics. Instead of peaceful coexistence, there would be chaos and disarray throughout the world. Western European countries, along with Canada, Australia and Japan, would form a united stand against this possible threat. The position of India in this scenario is difficult to predict at this time. If the leaders of China or Russia become power crazed and challenge the United States, these implications would simply be devastating. As things stand today, it seems unlikely.

With the present conditions prevailing in China, it is unlikely that the Chinese leaders will follow confrontational policies with the United States. The next ten years will make China more powerful in terms of its economy, as well as in its military superiority. The Chinese will not risk a war of words or missiles with the United States unless a dictator along the likes of Mao comes along. The United States and China know the strengths and weak points of the other. As of now, Taiwan could pose a thorny situation. The solution or solutions could be as simple as ignore it, maintain the status quo, or to resolve it peacefully. Either way, it will not be easy. With its robust economic growth, China is gaining global influence at unprecedented levels. Very soon it may challenge the United States and its global power. Both of these countries could live together side by side peacefully. Still, the other possibility might be to settle for a truce, with no real animosity, outside of a war of words, on occasion. Peaceful coexistence is naturally the best solution.

Relations with Mexico

Mexico is a fast emerging country. As a member state of NAFTA (North American Free Trade Alliance), it will play a very important role in the North American socio-economical and political arena. Presently, almost eleven percent of the U.S population consists of Spanish speaking people. Many of them are illegal immigrants. Naturally, Mexican immigration is a big problem. Will building a dividing wall between the two countries solve the problem? It might lessen the flow of illegal immigrants. However, it will not stop the migration. Economic disparity as well as other daily life factors between these two countries will continue to invite local Mexicans to the prosperity of the United States. Will this situation change in the next ten years? Probability dictates that it will not. If everything goes well with the Mexican economy, and if the drug kings do not destabilize the government, this would produce better chances that there would be fewer incentives for Mexican workers to migrate to the United States.

This notion holds true if there is good foreign investment in the economy and there is less corruption in the governing circle. Most importantly, it holds true if there is a brilliant, dedicated, forward-looking group of national leaders who can make the difference. There will be more investments from United States and other countries in the next ten years. However, Mexico requires a huge investment to turn the tide of poverty and unemployment. We do not see this arriving hastily in the coming decades. There is a high growth of population and there are no big increases in education facilities, health care, and Industrialization for the country as a whole. The relations of United States with Mexico are tied with the economic situation in Mexico. There will be friction and problems in the coming decade between these two countries, but not to extent of immigration issues that exist in today's conditions.

When NAFTA came into affect, it was thought that it would help Mexico in terms of large business opportunities, but this did not happen. Yes, there was a significant improvement in trade between the United States and Mexico, but not a spectacular one. There was no large inflow of foreign capital to Mexico and the country did not see rapid industrialization. The important sectors of education, drug eradication, health programs, and other social programs have not made any large progress. The United States government has to face the perennial problem of illegal immigration and there are no easy solutions. The Spanish speaking population has yet to arrive at the top layers of the American society; the majority of them are still struggling. Still, there exist exceptions, and the future looks brighter than it was few decades ago.

The United States and Japan

The present relations between the United States and Japan are close and friendly. The foreign policy of Japan runs parallel to the American point of view. As the second most powerful economic power in the world, Japan can play a very important role in the global politics. However, Japan's role as a military power is very limited. Its constitution prohibits it to become a nuclear power or engage in military build up. The past history of Japan, its occupation of mainland China, Korea and Taiwan are stumbling blocks for it to become a dominant force in Southeast Asia, even though China and Korea have established strong commercial relations with the nation.

In the next ten years, the business connections will continue to grow between these countries. However, the rising status of China in terms of economic wealth and military strength poses threat to the dominance of the United States in that part of the world. It is apparent that the United States will look towards Japan to help support its policy goals. Since the security of Japan is guaranteed by the United States against external forces, Japan will probably prove willing to support the United States when we look at matters of global policy. If the Chinese government takes up an aggressive anti-U.S. stand in the coming decade, there are strong indications that Japan and the U.S. will become closer in their foreign policy. The U.S. would like to maintain its supremacy in that part of the world and containing Chinese influence will become an important part of the U.S. global policies.

Taiwan is a hot spot in the world, today. The Peoples Republic of China claims Taiwan as an integral part of their nation. However, Taiwan has existed as an independent country since 1949. Very recently, in January of 2010, the U.S. agreed to sell military hardware worth around 7 billion dollars to Taiwan. China raised hell, warning Washington that its action will harm the Sino-American relations. Washington's position is to support the democratic government of Taiwan. Yet, if push comes to shove and China invades Taiwan, how the American government is going to react? China knows it very well that it cannot afford to take a direct hit from the military of the United States. In that scenario, Japan is certainly going to side with the United States as well. Another tricky situation may arise soon with the rising influence of China in Southeast Asia and in Africa. How will the U.S. attempt to contain China? The United States will not leave its territories of influence without a challenge. It seems very pertinent under these conditions that the United States would like to woo India.

Relations between Two Great Democracies: The United States and India

The world's greatest and largest democracies are the United States and India. During President Kennedy's time, India and U.S.A enjoyed a cordial, if not very friendly relationship. The American ambassador Professor Galbraith had built up a good rapport with the then Indian Prime Minister Nehru. Besides their friendship, Kennedy himself attached great importance to an Indian alliance. When China attacked India in 1962, U.S.A came to India's aid. However, after Kennedy's death, things started drifting in other directions. During Nixon's era, Indo-American relations became sour. Dr. Kissinger and President Nixon were anti-India and pro-China. Indian relations were excellent with Soviet Russia at that time. China, under Chairman Mao, was struggling with a cultural revolution and the situation seemed unthinkable. Nixon and Kissinger were very much interested in cultivating good relations with China, and thus they were ready to discard friendly relationship with India. Even Pakistan became more important than India. As China started gaining greater economical success, President George W. Bush felt that they have to change their policy towards India. It was a strategic foreign policy breakthrough. The friendship between India and the United States carries a very important global influence. If we look at these two countries in terms of cultural, economical, technological, religious freedom/tolerance, type of government, and other areas of comparison, it can be concluded that it is in the best interest of both countries to establish solid and friendly relations.

The people of India are proud to say that their country is the largest democracy in the world. The present mood of the countrymen is highly favorable towards the United States.

Historically speaking, it was President Bill Clinton who established friendly and closer relations between the United States and India. Nixon was, as stated before, anti-India to some extent. President Carter's mother had done some good social work in India, but he did not make any large effort to bring India closer to the United States. Regan had taken somewhat of a neutral stance. In India, there is a lot of admiration for what the United States stands for, and what it can offer to any ordinary citizen. The last two decades have shown that the Indians who have settled down in the United States have achieved remarkable success in all walks of life. People, who have come to the United States mostly as students, belong to middle and upper-middle class in India. The majority of them are professional, highly educated, and technical people. Like any other, they want to achieve the American Dream. The present Governor of Louisiana, Mr. Jindal, is an Indian-American citizen. Many Indians have risen to higher positions in the private sector, teaching institutions, and in socio-economic fields. There are about 1.6 million people of Indian origin who are living in the United States at present. With this background, we can say with good confidence that the future relations between these two countries will move towards more friendly and closer relationship.

According to the current Prime Minister of India, Dr. Man Mohan Singh, President George W. Bush was very keen on establishing closer relations with India. With the present world political situation, where China is emerging fast as a potential superpower, the United States has to look towards India as a nation that could challenge China militarily, economically and demographically in the region. Currently, China is ahead of India in all these categories. However, it can catch up soon, and both of these nations have the potential to become superpowers and potential enemies. Presently, the Chinese and Indian governments downplay any such scenario, both stating that the countries might coexist peacefully, side by side. The next ten years could solve Sino-Indian borders problems. Alternatively it might linger on; then, it could aggravate the situation. Depending on this, the relations between the United States and India will take shape. Another factor will be China and the Taiwan issue. If China tries to make Taiwan its own territory, there would be reaction from the United States. The nuclear energy treaty between the United States and India is another important consideration to think about. We feel the United States of America and India would move more towards closer and friendlier relationship in the next decade.

United States and France

How national leaders can change the direction of the relationship between countries is exemplified by the present President of France, Mr. Sarkozy. In a few months time, the chilly relations between France and United States were transformed because of him. He openly said that he admires the American people, their work ethics, and their entrepreneurship. He was invited to address the joint session of the U.S. Congress and was given a standing ovation. The days of President Chirac were forgotten. A new chapter has been opened for closer ties between the United States and France. Former President George W. Bush praised Mr. Sarkozy for taking these initiatives. The last ten years of U.S-France relationship were not cozy, but a new foundation has been laid now which could change the course for closer and friendly relations between these two countries moving forward. However, we must remember, a single person cannot change the perception of the whole nation. The people of France would have to change too. France is a global power; it has its own national priorities and interests. The French people are very proud of their culture, their language, and their heritage. Under these conditions, it will take some time before the ordinary French citizens will change their attitude, their thinking, and their liking or disliking for Americans. The next ten years for Franco-American relations will be dictated by an understanding and appreciation of each others' points of view, starting from the top government leaders and flowing through the general public.

Relations between United States and the Muslim World

Some of the most important Muslim countries of the world are Pakistan, a nuclear power, Saudi Arabia, the richest oil country, Indonesia, the most populated Muslim country, and Jordan-a close ally, Egypt, Iraq, Iran, and Afghanistan. Let us look at Pakistan first. Billions of dollars have been distributed to the Pakistan government headed by President Musharraf by the United States since 1999 to fight terrorism and Al Qaeda. The results have so far been dismal. The money was utilized to improve the status of the Pakistan army and the military personnel. The war against Al Qaeda in Afghanistan will not succeed until the abject poverty of the Afghan people is eliminated. Afghans are fierce fighters; independent minded and religious people. They will not live under a foreign regime. The United States and other European powers may not succeed in their efforts to root out terrorism and Al Qaeda forces unless the

Afghan people, as a whole, see better living conditions for themselves. Massive monetary resources are needed to make this happen. Will the European countries and the United States take on this huge burden? There is the likelihood that they will not. It seems the United States will continue to depend upon Pakistan to achieve its goal in the next ten years.

The second most important Muslim country is Saudi Arabia. It is changing a little bit as far as modernization is concerned. However, it will take decades before its ordinary citizen will be able to lead a contemporary life. The U.S depends upon the Saudi oil and the Saudis need American arms and aircrafts. The two countries will continue to move in the same fashion as they have been moving for the last ten years. We do not see any big difference in their relationship in the coming decade. The Jordanian kingdom will continue to be a good ally of the United States, perhaps the most important one.

United States and Afghanistan

At the invitation of the Prime Minister of Afghanistan, the Russians invaded the country in 1979. They stayed until 1989, when they were defeated by the combined forces of Islamist Militants, Mujahedeen, Afghani Taliban, and soldiers trained by the Pakistani forces. During this period, the Soviets spent a good amount of money to establish a communist country, but it was a disappointing failure. The Afghani people could not accept the concept of a Godless society. Simultaneously, the American government provided arms and money to the Pakistani government to flush out the Russian influence from Afghanistan. It was a success for United States diplomacy. In other words, Pakistan's army established the first group of the Afghani and Pakistani Taliban. Even today, Pakistan's Intelligence Services (I.S.I) supports Afghanistan's Taliban group.

Just after 9/11, President Bush announced the invasion of Afghanistan to destroy Al-Qaeda and eliminate Osama bin Laden. Afghanistan was a safe haven for Al-Qaeda and Osama. Though the American army defeated the Taliban and hoisted the regime of President Karzai, it has been a far from a complete success. In all practicality, the Taliban remains entrenched in the country and even after eight years, they are the de facto rulers of Afghanistan.

Presently, the country has become the largest supplier of drugs such as heroin, cocaine, and other narcotics. The farmer does not grow vegetables, he grows drug plants. It is one of the most disturbing situations; it is going to create lot of problems for the government moving forward.

Future Assessments

There are number of crucial situations that will dictate the future of the Afghan people and their relations with the outside world. The two most important factors are related to the presence of Al Qaeda's militants and of Taliban Jihadists; they are the arch enemies of the American interests. If the American military along with the NATO forces is able to dislodge and destroy these two groups, it will be a great victory.

The next step will be to establish an affective and competent Afghani military force to insure the safety and security of its people. A corrupt free central government will be essential if they are to make these changes. The United States and the Western powers will play the most important part in making these things happen. It will require continuous support in terms of money and other related resources to provide education, health, and technical skills to the general public. Afghanistan has gone from one tragedy to another major disaster. The majority of the local people say: Leave us alone. We don't want Taliban; we don't want the Americans. If you are our friend help us in building our country to live in peace and prosperity. The American policy should center on this idea. There can be no doubt that the Taliban and Al Qaeda have to be wiped out or made ineffective to start this strategy. At the same time, monetary and other kinds of assistance must be furnished to the local citizens of the country to win over their support. Afghanistan's problems are not going to go away soon. The drug problem is a serious threat to the country as well as to the entire world. It has to be solved in a practical manner.

The future relations between United States and Afghanistan will be based upon the priorities set by the U.S government's tactical strategies and global political scenario. The situation is too fluid to make any concrete suggestion or prediction for the future

United States and Pakistan

During the cold war era, United States foreign policy was based upon establishing military alliances. The South East Asia Treaty Organization (SEATO) was set up to combat the Russian influence in Asia. Pakistan was a member of this organization. When Russia tried to bring Afghanistan in its sphere of influence, the United States did not like it. The Pakistani military and government became a strong ally while helping the United States defeat the Russian intentions. Ultimately, Russia had to abandon Afghanistan. The United States had needed Pakistani military collaboration in this war with Russia. In the mean time the Taliban, Afghanistan's militia group, tried to establish a radical Islamist government in Afghanistan. After Russia's withdrawal, the United States lost this interest with Afghanistan and close cooperation with Pakistan also became a secondary concern. When Al-Qaeda and Osama bin Laden emerged, the United States sought to continue their relationship Pakistan. Things changed after September 11th, 2001; the United States, once again wanted Pakistan on its side to fight the Jihadist-Islamic militia groups. General Musharraf decided to become a full fledged partner with America. Billions of dollars were given to Pakistan to eliminate the Taliban fighters and supporters.

In 2008, President Musharraf was removed and, at present, there is a democratically elected government headed by Pakistan's People Party leader Asif Zardari; he is the husband of late Benazir Bhutto, the most popular leader of Pakistan. The present government of Pakistan is facing lot of problems. The economy is crumbling and with it, the country's law and order situation is out of control. Every week or so, there is a bomb explosion or a Suicide bomber blowing him up. There is no security of life and property. The U.S government is helping Pakistan in all possible ways to fight and eliminate Pakistani and Afghani Taliban fighters. It is a tough situation that requires lots of diplomatic moves along with monetary resources. At the same time, majority of the general public of Pakistan is anti-American.

Future Assessments

The supportive role of Pakistan is very crucial for the United States in its quest to eliminate both Afghani and Pakistani Taliban forces, as well as Al Qaeda. Extreme radical groups in both countries have unleashed terror through out the world. It is a very difficult task; abject poverty, illiteracy, unemployment, drug problem and tribal rules, including Sharia laws, cannot be eradicated and removed in a short period of time. The United States along with their Western allies will have to work hard and spend the money and resources to overcome these serious problems. Looking from this perspective, it is easy to assume that there will a continuous close relationship between Pakistan and the United States in the near future and in the long run. Al Qaeda and the Taliban collectively have become a dangerous enemy and if they are not eliminated they could create lot of problems, not only for the United States but for the whole civilized world. It is true that economic problem and extreme fanatical religious views are the root causes for the acceptance of radical Islamic groups whether they are in Pakistan, Afghanistan or elsewhere. When a man has nothing to lose, he can do anything. This is the mentality of a suicide bomber. The next five years will be very critical for the safety of American interests as well as for other nations. The Taliban and Al Qaeda can be eliminated entirely, but it will take hard work and determination. It seems safe to say that Pakistan and the United States along with other Western countries will be working together for a long period of time as common allies.

United States and Iraq

When Saddam Hussein invaded Kuwait, former President George H.W. Bush got the United Nations' approval to go ahead and pursue military actions and Kuwait was liberated. He did not consider the option to invade Iraq. Things changed when his son, former President George W. Bush, became the chief commander of U.S. forces. After 9/11, the government of the United States decided to attack Iraq and dislodge Saddam's regime. It was a unilateral move; England supported it, Germany and France opposed it. Within a short period, Saddam's army was badly defeated and the United States occupied Iraq. Though Saddam's regime had collapsed, another war erupted in Iraq, a civil struggle between Sunnis and Shiites. In the past, the Sunnis Muslims were governing the country despite being the minority. Nearly seventy percent of the population is Shiites. This historical animosity between Sunnis and Shiites may lead to a civil war in Iraq. Every day, some bomb is exploded in a suicide attack; there is absolutely no safety of life and property.

The present conditions of Iraq are chaotic, unpredictable, and desperate. It is difficult to predict what future holds for Iraq. The current President of the United States, Barrack Obama, wants to pull out all the troops from Iraq within a year or two. It has been assumed by the present administration that the Iraqi military will be able to take control and handle the situations of law and order in the country before the American forces withdraw from Iraq. No doubt, there will be some military presence to help the Iraqi forces. There is also no secret that the Iraqis do not like the American presence in their country.

Future Assessments

The invasion of Iraq by the United States resulted in some very catastrophic results for Iraq, for the United States, and for the rest of the world. It dismantled a dictatorship, introduced a democratic set up for the country, and created divisionary forces between Sunnis and Shiites. The Iraqi war cost billions of dollars to the American government and thousands of American soldiers lost their lives. It changed the Iraqi life, but perhaps not for the better. Property worth billions of dollars was destroyed and nearly a million Iraqis died in the war.

The majority of the people all around the world think that it was not worth the cost of fighting such a war. President George W. Bush made a terrible mistake. What was done cannot be undone now. It will take a long time for Iraqi people to like the United States and its people. A permanent mark of bitter hostility and aversion may prevail towards America. There may never be a feeling of closeness between the Iraqis and the Americans, at least for the foreseeable few decades. Time heals everything though and gradually these wounds might heal as well.

The invasion of Iraq also brought about a distinct polarization of Muslims against the Americans and Western culture. It has created a feeling of unease and discomfort between Muslim community and others. Muslims have feelings of distrust against Christians, Hindus, Jews, and other religions. They feel that the Western culture is out to destroy the Muslim way of life.

Suicide bombers and Muslim militants have sprung all over the world; they want to destroy normal, peaceful life wherever they can. The Palestine problem and the Iraqi episode have united the Muslim world to some extent. American and European diplomacy should attempt to dispel the notion that Muslim countries and the rest of the world cannot live together. It does require lot of patience, education, and lot of resources.

The United States and Iran, the Evil Empire

The Shah of Iran was thrown out in 1969 and the cleric Khomeni became the most powerful man in the country, assuming an almost king-like status and rule. The Shah did not realize that the ordinary person of the street was capable of such a revolution. During the time of the Shah, the United States was a close ally of Iran. Things changed after Khomeni came to power. President George W. Bush called Iran and North Korea the Axis of Evil, or essentially evil empires. Today, the present President of Iran is anti-U.S. to the core; he does not mince any words in naming the United States as the most obnoxious country globally. With this background, along with the friendly relations between Iran, Russia, and China, the Western countries and the United States are facing a tough dilemma.

Iran wants to become a nuclear power, the main issue as of right now. Furthermore, Iran has declared openly that it will use the nuclear power against Israel if it feels that it is needed. Iranian government is openly defying the political pressure from the European countries and the United States. The President of the United States has threatened stiff sanctions against the Iranian government if it continues to go ahead with its nuclear plans. The United Nations is not in a position to stop the Iranian government's moves to enrich the uranium to make nuclear weapons. How does one stop these nations from achieving nuclear power?

Future Assessments

It seems that the present Iranian regime is trying to buy time before it could finally achieve its goals of becoming a nuclear power. Despite of all kinds of political pressure from the West, Iran is not budging from its position. If this process continues moving along, one of the possibilities could be drastic action from Israel that would destroy the potential nuclear facilities. It is difficult to predict what is going to transpire in this situation. With the backing of China and Russia, Iran may continue to go against the wishes of the Western world and the United States. In the long run, the relations between Iran and the United States seem tangential, without any meeting ground.

The Iranian government wants to lead the Muslim world. However, the majority of Muslim people are Sunnis while Iranians are Shiites; thus, they may not like the idea of being led by Shiites. The United States is trying to convince the Arabic Sunnis to stop the Iranians goals. Pakistan, already a nuclear power, is a Sunni state that enjoys good relations with the present Iranian government. Pakistan in the past has helped Iran and North Korea, but now the situation has changed because of Taliban problem in Pakistan and Afghanistan.

Lately, there has been some opposition to the religious leaders of Iran, the Ayatollahs and the Khomenis, but the chances of a revolt against the present regime are remote. An attack on Iran by the Israel or the United States will generate lot of upheaval in the Muslim world. It is clear that there is a polarizing atmosphere between the Muslim world and the rest of the world. It is unfortunate, but also true that most of the Muslim countries have high unemployment, lower literacy rates, and bad economic conditions. The United States of America can not solve these problems all by itself; the whole world may have to pitch in this effort. The future relations between Iran and the United States look bleak and dismal. It might similarly prove true that Iran might never achieve the status of being a nuclear power under these present conditions. The revolutionary government of Iran cannot be trusted.

United States and Israel

The government of the United States has supported Israel from its conception as a nation. It has become perhaps their biggest diplomatic problem; Muslim militants, suicide bombers, Jihadists, the Taliban, and Al Qaeda have all blamed the United States for extending solid support to Israel. Most of the Muslim countries are against the friendly relations that exist between Israel and the United States. Former Presidents Jimmy Carter and Bill Clinton had tried their best to bring Palestine and Israel towards peace, but ultimately both failed. Under the present circumstances, it has become very difficult to find a solution that would be acceptable to Palestine and Israel. Thus, the United States must face these kinds of problems on three fronts: Palestine, Afghanistan and Iraq. Under no condition will the United States abandon Israel.

Israel is a nuclear power and it has military superiority in all areas compared to Arab countries. In 1967, it has proved, beyond any doubt that it can defend itself without the help of any other country; though it must not be forgotten that the United States provides massive financial aid as well as military equipment to Israel.

THE FOREIGN POLICY OF THE UNITED STATES UNDER PRESIDENT OBAMA

President Obama has charted some new directions for United States foreign policy, specifically towards Muslim Countries as well as for other countries like North Korea, Brazil, Venezuela, Mexico, India, China, and Russia. Let us examine some of the details.

Most of the Muslim countries of the world consider the United States and other Western countries as anti-Islamic in their assessments. This view has been reinforced after the American invasion of Iraq and Afghanistan. President Obama wants o remove this notion that the United States is anti-Islamic. President George W. Bush had also tried to correct this situation, but there was no change in the public opinion by Muslim nations with regards to America.

Obama went all the way to Egypt to address the Muslim world. He openly declared that the United States is not anti-Islamic, and that it wants to establish friendly relations with the Muslim world. In a recent survey conducted in Muslim countries to find out if Obama's efforts made any difference in the opinions of the Muslim population, it has been reported that no significant change was noticed. The general public of the Muslim countries still distrust the Americans and they are still anti-American. In other words, President Obama's personal efforts did not make any big difference. Seventy percent population of Pakistan, Afghanistan, Palestine, Iraq, Iran, Indonesia and Malaysia remain opposed to America.

People think that Obama might not be anti-Islamic, as his father was a Muslim, but most of the Americans are not Muslims and therefore Muslim nations see that he does not perhaps truly represent the nation as a whole. The survey report further pointed out that there is no change of heart towards women in the Muslim societies, as far as the influences of the Taliban and Al Qaeda are concerned. All the slogans and government efforts to change their treatment of women was of no real use. This should be an eye opener for the American government. History tells us that changes do not come easy and it takes time and constant effort to make it happen. This might be very true of many Muslim nations and societies. Will Obama be able to win over the confidence of the Muslim world? The chances are not likely, but his movement is in the right direction.

Economic conditions and education will be the primary driving forces to make these changes; the political changes will not be able to make things happen alone. The United States and other Western countries should devote their resources in this direction to see greater, more positive results. Otherwise it will be just a waste of money and time.

It is no surprise that the American attack on Iraq was a big mistake, fueling the flames of mistrust and hatred of America in the Muslim world. Before Iraq, Palestine was the main source of anti-American sentiment because of their support of Israel. It is the kind of hatred and distrust that starts building up when economic conditions, high unemployment rate, lack of education, and technical training can be found in abundance in a society. The views of Taliban and Al Qaeda can be changed by providing jobs, technical and business training, a 21st century view of the world, food and shelter, education, and good health facilities for the general public. It is not easy; it will require tremendous resources and persistent efforts to make these transformations. The Western countries in accordance with the United States have to consider how and when these changes can be brought about, as well as who will be taking charge of it. Lot of training will be required by the local communities to make it a success.

Relations with India and China

The United States and India began to establish good relations under the presidency of George W. Bush. India's Prime Minister, Man Mohan Singh, and Mr. Bush were instrumental in sealing the nuclear deal that helped India acquire the latest technical understandings of nuclear technology. The United States also agreed to help in the setting up of nuclear power plants in India. This nuclear deal has drawn the two countries together for larger business transactions. India has shown interest in purchasing military planes and other armaments from the

United States. It is a pact that has brought the two countries a little bit closer in terms of trade and political alignments. There was some speculation that former President Bush was going out of his way to accommodate the Indian point of view. The reason given for this "inclination" was that America needs a balance for the growing influence of China in Southeast Asia, and this could be accomplished with India on its side. This is a very important consideration in the realm of global politics.

It is true that India and China are strong competitors. Pretty soon they will be able to replace a lot of the Western European influence in the world power order. When Mr. Obama became the President, he announced some points in his foreign policy concerning Pakistan, Afghanistan, and India. The Indian government was concerned about massive financial aid that the United States had promised to Pakistan.

Further, there were speculations about the role of the United States as a third party by pass for improving relations between India and Pakistan. India does not want any third party involvement related to Kashmir and the other issues that have persisted between these two countries for a long period of time. Initially, it seemed that Obama was not going to be as close to India as Bush had been. This was the general perception, but the realities of his policy have yet to come to fruition.

Another point of importance for India is the H1 visas for Indian students. Due to the financial crisis in the United States, Obama wanted to restrict the visa, in addition to imposing certain conditions on the outsourcing of information technology projects to India and China. It was a matter of serious concern for the government of India because the United States is the biggest customer of Indian software programs. Outsourcing is a global phenomenon and putting restrictions on it could be termed as supporting protectionism. It would not be good for the country nor the rest of the world.

Recently, President Obama said that he would like to establish very close relations with China, relations that would shape the century. Former President Bush did not share this desire to become close with China. China has invested about a trillion of American dollars in U.S. Bonds and Treasury Bills. This is bound to influence any U.S President. The question is one where the president might be looking at China as a counter balance against Russia. The United States and China are bound to meet each other as dual superpowers at some point. How much interest the United States shows towards China has yet to truly be seen. What exactly Obama means when he says that it will shape the century has yet to come to any kind of concrete agreement or strategy. Given the meteoric rise of the Chinese economy, reasons for keeping friendly relations with China are obvious. The world will not be entangled in another Cold War since nobody is eager for that to happen again. China knows it pretty well that going against U.S.A would be disastrous for its own economy. There may still be verbal skirmishes between the two countries from time to time, but they probably would be trivial in nature. Thus, it is possible that, in addition to the U.S, Russia, China and India might also soon achieve the status of superpowers.

Iran and North Korea

Once a powerful ally, Iran is now one of the most anti-American nations. The present President of Iran, Ahmadijenad, is a revolutionary and a strong critic of Israel, Western countries, and the United States. As long as he is in power he is not going to budge from his nuclear plans. President Obama's overtures to him will probably not pay any dividends. Iran will continue to build up its nuclear program, and, like North Korea, it will continue to deflect any Western country's counter plans. North Korea wants and needs financial aid from the United States, but that is not true in the case of Iran. With booming oil prices, Iran has plenty of resources and is not looking for any financial assistance from the European Union or any other source. In the next decade or so, Iran will most probably achieve its status as a nuclear power.

Did Obama's change of policy towards Iran make any progress? Not at all, and there is no chance of getting any of the results that the United States and European Union are looking for. They could impose sanctions against Iran, but it will not yield any tangible results. It is very difficult to stop any nation from going nuclear unless you are ready to stage some kind of conflict to destroy the nuclear installations by bombardment. Israel has declared in the past that it will not hesitate to dismantle the Iranian nuclear sites once it feels that it has become a threat to its security.

The United States and the Western countries in such a situation should be ready to face the consequences of such action. There would be more anti-Western sentiment and continued Jihadist's suicide bombings. Would the Western countries handle this scenario or will they let Iran get their nuclear status? It is difficult to predict. It is one of the hot spots in the international political arena. It might be a battle between Israel and Iran and rest of the Muslim world. Russia may not openly support Iran's intentions, though it might not get involved in actively opposing it either. It has good relations with Iran and showing solidarity with its ambitions, Russia might gain something politically in the Muslim world.

North Korea, another country which possesses nuclear capabilities, is going through the rough times of poverty, unemployment, and starvation. Still, the dictator does not care and keeps on threatening the West with their nuclear program. According to expert opinion, North Korea is very close to becoming a nuclear power. China, Japan, Russia, the United States, South Korea and the United Nations are trying to put pressure on North Korea to dismantle its nuclear program. The government is contradictory: sometimes they claim they will stop, only to begin testing long range missiles to show to the world that they can be real threat to global security. It seems like they primarily want a good package of foreign aid to overcome the persistent shortage of food, housing, and other problems. They want a guarantee from the United States that would ensure a continuous flow of food and financial aid. It would thus appear to be in the interest of Western countries to help the North Korean government to overcome their present problems. China had been their close ally in the past, and South

Korea could help out the North Koreans provided they give up its nuclear ambitions. It seems that North Korea may give up its nuclear ambitions and may soon enter into some kind of agreement with Western nations and allies. President Obama has not changed the American policy as it pertains to North Korea.

Afghanistan and Pakistan

Afghanistan has gone from misery to greater misery, whether it was under Russian influence or under the American and European countries. All these years the general public has suffered from starvation, poverty, ill health, illiteracy, no jobs, and no real relief. The Afghanistan people know that their future is still very bleak and uncertain, despite the western countries that are pouring millions of dollars into their country to improve the lives of the ordinary person. Taliban and Al Qaeda still are very powerful forces in the daily life of the Afghani people. The immediate future generation of Afghanis faces a bleak future. It might take a few decades before the Afghani people can look beyond this state and see a prosperous future on the horizon.

With this background, let us examine what President Obama's foreign policy for Afghanistan and Pakistan hope to achieve. Obama has increased military personnel. He is extending a friendly hand towards moderate Taliban and Al Qaeda militants. Further, there has been an active participation of Pakistani forces to destroy the strongholds of Taliban and their supporters. The drug lords of Afghanistan are thriving and there is lot of corruption in the government machinery. The ordinary Afghani on the street does not care about the American forces fighting against the militants, Taliban, and suicide bombers. They are interested in knowing how the daily needs of ordinary people are going to be met. It is a grim situation.

The Afghani people are brave and are good fighters. They did not like the Russians and they do not seem to take kindly to the Western influence either. It will take a long time and it will require lot of resources to make Afghanistan a safe and desirable country to live in. If the Western countries are ready to provide massive economic aid, as well to establish educational and technical institutions to train the future generation of Afghan people, only then will we see a bright future for Afghanistan. It will be very difficult to wipe out Taliban and Al Qaeda organizations from the cross sections of Afghanistan society. It is deep rooted and well entrenched. The whole culture of the country has to change and it will not be easy. Obama's policy to crush Taliban and Al Qaeda in the near future will be difficult to achieve. Just as the Russians were defeated, the Western countries, along with the United States, might find themselves in a very precarious position in spite of massive military strength.

President Obama's policies towards Pakistan are very well defined in the sense that they are result oriented. The U.S government wants to see results and actions. The Pakistan military is well entrenched in Pakistani politics and democratically elected presidents and prime ministers will not be able to dislodge its powerful position. Keeping this in mind, the Western nations and the United States have to work very closely with the Pakistani military leaders. The military generals will do only things that work well and coincide with their own self interest. They know that they can replace an elected government with a bloodless coup and without much fuss from the people. These generals have ruled over Pakistan for almost thirty years. The situation in Pakistan is not as grim as in Afghanistan.

CHAPTER 3

United Kingdom

Great Britain once ruled almost half the world. The sun never set on its empire. They find themselves in a position that is different now. The devastating effects of World War II changed the whole global power spectrum. Still, it maintains its status as a great country, a rich country that is highly industrialized, and a nuclear power. There are more than fifty countries which are members of the Commonwealth. Queen Elizabeth is not only one of the richest women but also a very popular figure throughout the world. The British people are highly disciplined, hard working, and smart. Presently, the gross national income for a British citizen is around $45,000. The population is around sixty two million.

What does the future unfolds for this country? What does the next decade holds in store for this once glorious, rich and mighty powerful nation? Let us first examine the population trends. One finds all kinds of nationalities settled down in England. London is extremely diverse. There are about two million Indians, more than one millions Pakistani, and about one million Bangladeshi living in England. There are few millions from the African continent that now, take up residence in Britain.

In ten years, it is likely this segment of the population will increase. The British population will go up as well, but to a smaller degree. To assimilate all the cross sections of the population will not be an easy task for the British government, but it can and must be done. It will depend upon many factors; job opportunities will be one of the major factors. If the British economy keeps on moving forward, this will be a lesser problem. However, social and cultural differences will also be a big part in the assimilation process.

Gradually, British society is moving more towards American way. However, there is a big difference. The society is divided into many hierarchies, such as the royal family, the family of Lords, big established barons of wealth and fame, middle class and the working class, the blue class and so on. This makes it slightly more difficult for the government to enforce laws that favor the common man. It is reported by some media sources that House of Lords would be abolished and in its place, might someday, be an elected Senate, a highly democratic move.

FUTURE DIRECTIONS FOR THE ECONOMY

More and more highly industrialized countries of the West are moving from the manufacturing base to that of service sector, a trend that is already occurring in England and likely to accelerate in the future. London is the largest financial market in Europe. Just as with the U.S., it seems likely that the United Kingdom will keep its sophisticated manufacturing industries intact. All other kinds of production industries will continue to drift to the emerging countries of Europe and Asia. Is this good for the country? Regardless of any consideration, we notice that it is a world wide phenomenon. Same kind of business conditions are prevailing in Japan as well. China and India will emerge as two large manufacturing bases in the near future. The next decade will see the world evolve more through cooperation and globalization rather than isolation when we compare with the last ten years.

MILITARY SUPERIORITY

Even today, England is a top military power. It seems likely that it will continue to be such in the forthcoming decade. In the context of population, at around sixty million, England is far behind China, India, the United States and Russia. Quantity does matter; despite the effects that nuclear power might have in a long drawn out war. Small, regional wars need sophisticated conventional weapons, not nuclear missiles. In this respect, United Kingdom would be ahead of many countries, with conventional armaments that are sophisticated and advanced.

EXISTING AND FUTURE RELATIONS
WITH OTHER COUNTRIES

United Kingdom and France

The new President of France, Mr. Sarkozy, is turning a new chapter by establishing more cordial and friendly relationship with England. It is a turning point, compared to the days of Mr. Chirac's presidency. It again illustrates how the personal chemistry between national leaders plays such an important role in nurturing and sustaining relations between nations. However, it will take some time for the people of the concerned countries to adjust their attitude and reactions towards the other country.

The foundation of friendlier relations between England and France will become more solid, based on many factors. The British government has so far kept itself rather isolated from the European Union. It still has its own currency intact, as well as keeping their immigration rules and regulations independent. Mr. Sarkozy wants the United Kingdom to become more involved in the European Union.

France has to have more Presidents like Mr.Sarkozy in order for England to become more cooperative with the E.U. in coming years. The Iraqi War has been a thorny issue between France and England. England does not think twice about its policy matters when it is concerned with the United States. Historically, the United States and the United Kingdom have stood side by side most of the time and there are strong indications that they will continue to flourish as such. What about France? With Presidents like Sarkozy sitting on the French side, there is no reason for England not to become more involved in the E.U. and develop a mutually beneficial relationship with France. It will be a slow yet steady journey that might take some time.

England and Germany

Hitler and World War II are not easy to forget though more than sixty years have passed. Like anything else, those dark days will eventually be erased to some extent. The present relations between England and Germany are not cold, though they are far from very close. There are no areas of conflict at the present time. Germany is not a nuclear country and is no longer a military power. The people of Germany have to show to the world that the past is gone for good and that the new Germany could be counted on to promote the welfare of the lesser developed nations of the world. It will depend upon the German people and its leaders to come out from its past and help in building a better tomorrow for the entire world. More cooperation between the people of other countries and Germany will serve as a good start. Close relations between Germany and England in the next ten years are not difficult to achieve. However, the common grounds to build that relationship are not as readily prevalent as they are between the U.K. and France. It seems that Germans are closer to the people of France than to the British. What will happen in the next decade is, at this point, a matter of speculation.

Relations between England and Russia

Prime Minister Margret Thatcher told the world that she could do business with the Russian President Gorbachev. American President Ronald Regan followed her lead. It was the beginning of a thaw between the two superpowers and between the USSR and the West. The relations between communist Russia and Western countries started warming up steadily. After Gorbachev, President Boris Yeltsin became a close friend of President Bill Clinton and the then German Chancellor. After Yeltsin, President Putin started a journey of cozy personal relations with the British and other Western countries. At the end of his president term however, Mr. Putin began to resume Cold War rhetoric. By this time, Russia had changed quite a bit.

The soaring high prices of oil and gas have started bringing huge sums of money into the Russian economy. As it looks now, strains have started surfacing between Russia and Western countries, including the United States. In the recent past, some Russian diplomats were asked to leave England for espionage amongst other charges. There are differences between Russia and America over the American missile plan in Europe. Mr. Putin strongly opposes it. The Russian leaders realize that though Russia is a great Nuclear power- second only to the United States-yet the country is far behind Western countries in terms of gross national income. Their per capita income is $9,000 compared to $45,000 gross national income of England.

In terms of military superiority, Russia is far ahead of England and has the backing of a larger population. How the future governments of Russia and its leaders will align their foreign policies with Western countries is difficult to predict due to the high number of variables. It seems that Russian leadership will make it clear to Western countries that they can not take Russia for granted as a permanent ally.

There exists a strong likelihood of minor differences and a minute possibility of some major policy differences in the next decade. It can be safely predicted that the British policy as it relates to Russia will not differ from that of the United States

England and Australia

Australia and Canada recognize the Queen of England as their own queen. All these three countries have historical bonds and are very close to each other. The standard of living of Australians is as good as that of a British citizen; their GNI is roughly $43,000 per capita. Australia's population is around twenty million people. Look from a broad perspective: Australia is a sub continent; a big country; it has a huge area of land that could be used to settle new immigrants; it should increase its population through large scale of immigration; raise its military strength and become a giant economical power.

At one point, there was a movement to declare Australia as a republic, but this did not gain substantial momentum.

Presently, the trade relations of Australia are strongly tied with the Asian countries because of the geographical proximity. China and Japan are the leading trading partners of Australia.

Long time ago- 1930-60, Asian immigrants were not allowed in Australia; it followed what was called the "White Only" policy. But things have changed, and presently the Asian community is welcomed. The foreign policy of Australia follows, more or less, the same direction as England's policy.

Unlike England, Australia is not a military power and therefore does not carry any real weight in the realm of global politics. Would the future ten years be similar to what they are presently, with regards to their mutual relationship? The answer is, most probably yes. These two countries do not have any serious conflicting issue that would warrant a change.

Like many other Western European countries, Australia will move along the same lines economically and culturally, similar to England. Australia cannot catch up with super military powers unless it becomes a nuclear power and experiences a growth in population.

England and the United States will come to Australia's help if ever there is any danger to its sovereignty. However, there are some very distinct differences between Australia and England. Australia, at this point in time, can absorb lot of immigrants, both Asian and European, in order to play a more dominant role in global politics. For it to spend money and other resources on armaments would not be a smart move. Yes, it can and should expand its industry base. Presently, it is a big exporter of iron ore, coal, gas, uranium, etc. and has large manufacturing as well as service industries.

The ex Prime Minister of Australia, Mr. Rudd was thinking on those lines of thought and was formulating policies in that direction-expansion plans through liberal immigration policies especially for Asians. Surprisingly, Prime Minister Kevin Rudd lost his position as Prime-Minister and now is the Foreign Minister of Australia. This change in political hierarchy would either abandon or delay indefinitely the Expansion Plans.

Relations between England and India

Relations between England and India have many facets. They are evolving in new directions as the world is changing. We have to start from the colonial past; England ruled over India for almost two hundred years. English is one of the official languages of free India and most of the middle class in Indian society use English in their daily lives. Many of the cultural values have British flavor. Most of the pre-independent Indian political leaders were educated in prestigious English Universities. What was the British attitude in the early days of the colonial era? An attitude of superiority and arrogance towards Indians was prevalent, but as times have changed so has the attitude changed. However, there are still some hardcore groups of people who look down upon Indians and still consider themselves superior in many ways.

We cannot change the world. There are all kinds of people; education, global exposure, interaction with other societies and understanding other people's culture, all of these and many other factors go hand in hand to make this world a better place. The first Prime Minister of India, Mr. Nehru, laid a good foundation for better relations with England. India's Father of the Nation, Mahatma Gandhi, had deep respect for many of the moral and spiritual values held by the British people. The first migration of Indian people in England consisted mostly of labor, non-technical and the non-educated class. Later on, doctors, highly educated, and technical savvy people migrated. They were of the middle and the upper-middle class section of Indian society.

These people demanded respect from the local British colleagues and from the general public. Life has changed for many Indians who are living in England now. Life is still a second class for others. This could be explained by considering an example of Indian migrants who are doing very well in the United States. Higher education, technical knowledge, business training, adaptability, assimilation in the local community and a dream to succeed are some of the most important attributes that propelled these migrants to the top of the American financial, educational, social, and political charts. If the people of Indian origin in England follow their American counterparts, there is no reason for them not to quickly ascend to similar success in England.

There are almost two million Indians living in England now. It will require effort from the individuals as well as from the government to change the situation for those who are unfortunately going nowhere. The last ten years have seen healthy and friendly relations between England and India. British Prime Minister Tony Blair was a friend of India and the present Prime Minister Gordon Brown has excellent relations with the present Prime Minister of India, Dr. Man Mohan Singh. The Indian business leaders like Mr. Ratan Tata and others have invested heavily in the British industry and British investment in India is on the rise. The people in India and England have started a two way street of business prosperity and mutual appreciation. Ten years from now, the relations between these countries will be closer than they are today unless some major problem comes along. There are few chances of it.

England and China

The relations between China and England are what we can call "normal". There are no issues of conflict. However, things could change; notably, if there is an open confrontation between Taiwan and China. United States and England would react with sharp and calculated retributions. If China starts a war against India, England would definitely support Indian interests. China and England are maintaining good business relations via Hong Kong. Lots of foreign direct investment in China comes through big investment firms located there.

It is the United States, Japan, and Australia that are leading trading partners with China and not England. Most of the military weapons for the Chinese army are supplied by the Russians, and not by England or United States. There are lots of Chinese people who live in United States as opposed to England. China does not consider England a nation capable of threatening their power, unlike United States. There is a keen competition between United States and China, but that is not so between China and England. Looking at the past ten years of history, it seems that the relations between these two countries will move along on a positive note in the coming decade.

England and Japan

After World War II was over, the world had already changed. New relations were started between countries that were once fierce enemies. The relations between Japan and Western countries started gradually- became healthy and prosperous. After sixty years, these relations have taken strong roots. Japan is a firm ally of the United States and other Western nations, including England. As with China, England does not have any dispute with the Japanese government. The trade relations are moving along on a normal pace between these two countries. Since Japan is no longer a military power, there are no military connections of any kind. However, there are some movements in Japan that want to amend its constitution and expand the role of its military. This might change the position. The next ten years of relationship between England and Japan will likely be positive and cordial

England and Pakistan

Relations between England and Pakistan are based upon four basic conditions. They are the dictatorship in Pakistan; terrorism and the presence of Al Qaeda, assimilation of Pakistani migrants in British society, and the nuclear status of Pakistan. Pakistan has been governed by the military dictators for almost thirty years, out of a total of roughly sixty years of independence. These dictators ruled the country with an iron fist mentality, and it has made them rich in the process. The masses of the country have remained in poverty. The result was the rise of terrorism and the greater influence of Al Qaeda and Taliban insurgents, beginning in the tribal area of Pakistan and extending to the mainland.

Another important consideration in the English –Pakistani relationship has been the assimilation of Pakistani migrants into British society. A few years ago, young Pakistani members of terrorist groups put bombs in the trains and buses of London. More than fifty people died in those attacks. These terrorists were trained in Pakistan. Since Pakistan is a nuclear power it adds up another threatening element.

All these and other socio-economic and educational considerations have assumed paramount importance for their present and future relations. It seems that Pakistan will move between their military dictatorship and a democratic set up in the future. The military is too powerful a force there. The British government has to deal with this scenario and it will not be easy. The present Prime Minister of England Mr.David Cameron raised a political uproar by publicly stating that Pakistani Government exports terrorism to other countries. The reality is that the present Pakistan's government is unable to control terrorists and militants in their country and these groups plan and stage terrorist activities in other countries like India, England and the United States. England is providing a large amount of financial aid to Pakistan to overcome its multi faced problems. England has become the political base of Pakistan's politicians.

England and Canada

Canada has strong ties with England and Queen Elizabeth is the Queen of Canada as well. Historically, Canada has had a strong connection with France. In 1967, General DeGaulle declared : Long live free Quebec. In 2006, the present Prime Minister of Canada, Mr. Stephen Harper made the province of Quebec a nation, within Canada. This was a political friendly gesture towards separatist Quebec majority and nothing more because nothing has changed drastically. The separatist movement of Quebec ended in 2003 when the Party Quebecoise was defeated. Canada acquired full autonomy from England in 1931 and in 1947 became an equal partner of England. It was in 1967 that Canada became a full fledged independent country in all aspects. It is an important member of the Commonwealth and a home for many British citizens. The population of Canada is 32 million strong with a GNI around $43,000 per capita.

Prime Minister Trudeau supported immigration from Asian countries and was a very popular and charismatic liberal leader. There was an initial resistance against the Asian immigrants that has since melted away. The Asian community, especially Indians and Chinese immigrants, are doing very well in Canada. However, there are pockets of unequal opportunity that still prevail in some quarters; we hope that will fade away with time.

The globalization effect is changing the attitudes and behavior of all the communities of the world. There is no country or people who could boast about their superiority because every nation and its people can move to the top position and the concept of a monopoly or superiority is disappearing as the world and the technologies are moving too fast to delve into such silly notions.

Just as England and the United States are very close so are the relations between England and Canada. We should note that Canada lacks military superiority; it is not a nuclear power and it does not have the advantage of a huge population. If Canada opens its doors more generously to immigrants, there is a good chance that it will acquire a stronger and important position in global politics.

Ten years from now, we see no reason for England and Canada not to continue their friendly and close relationship. Canada offers a good meeting ground of people from British heritage as well as those who have French connections. At the present juncture, there are very remote chances of a separate Quebec state. Canada would be a strong nation of British and French speaking people.

England and Iraq

Tony Blair, the former British Prime Minister, had supported President Bush all the way to remove Saddam's regime. The general public of England was not in favor of the British policies in Iraq. The unilateral policy of President Bush to invade Iraq was criticized by most of the countries of the world, including many in Britain. It has created a lot of complex situations, especially by creating a world that is seemingly segregated between Muslim and non-Muslim worlds. The British Muslim population has grown polarized against the present British policies and many of them have joined the Jihadist/Militant Islamic groups. This is true of many British citizens of Pakistani origin. The present policies of England would be to support the local Iraqi government, similar to the policies of the United States, both monetarily and in other areas. The British troops will undoubtedly be out of Iraq pretty soon

England and Iran

The present president of Iran, Mr. Admadinejad, is a radical Islamist follower. He is creating difficulties for the United States and other Western countries regarding their nuclear plan. Israel and most of the West contend that the Iranians are planning to build nuclear weapons, while the Iranian government denies it. It is true that a nuclear Iran could be a big security threat not only to Israel but to the whole world because of its past terrorist-related policies. Russia and China are against imposing any sanctions on Iran. England, like other Western countries, is worried about the real motive of the Iranian government. The general public of Iran is anti-West, anti-U.S., and they do want the country to have a nuclear arsenal to fight against Israel. It is a sticky global situation. If it is not resolved peacefully, it might have very serious repercussions. England and Iran's relations with the present cleric regime will not be cozy and friendly as long as the Iranians keep on pursuing their nuclear dreams.

England and Afghanistan

President Karzai needs all the help he can get to contain Taliban and Al Qaeda. England is a member of the NATO forces in Afghanistan. To eliminate Taliban and Al Qaeda from Afghanistan is not an easy task. It will take a massive effort to help the local Afghani people in terms of jobs, technical training, farming, etc. so that they can stand on their own feet and gradually dissipate these two groups. Military action is not the only and absolute solution. The country has seen the worst human crisis in recent years and the world should come to its aid. England's policies towards Afghanistan will be to help the government in all areas of operations, ranging from education, health, military training, industrialization, and so on. This holds true for the United States and other countries that are willing to help the country to stand on its feet. It is a long road; there are no other alternatives. The war against extremism and terrorism can only be won, not solely by fighting, but through economic assistance and education. This war will be won by the cooperation of the local people; the outsiders alone will not be able to hoist peace on the turbulent landscape.

England and Arab Countries

England has maintained very friendly relations with Saudi Arabia. Very recently, the Saudi king stayed with the Queen of England as a special guest. The Saudis are good customers of England through their purchase of military supplies from British companies. The British army helps in training Saudi's soldiers. This mutually beneficial relationship between the Saudis and the United Kingdom will continue in future.

The present President of Syrian studied in England and he is well versed in European way of life. Syria supports Hamas, an organization that has been labeled as a terrorist outfit by the United States government. We can say, though with some reservations, that Syria is anti-American, but neutral towards England.

England has maintained friendly relations with Jordan. Late King Hussain was married to a British wife. He had attended the British Military Academy. He was on very good terms with the Queen of England. Jordan has maintained friendly relations with the U.S. and other western countries including the United Kingdom. Egypt also falls under this category; it is also the only Arabic country that maintains diplomatic relations with Israel

CHAPTER 4

Republic of India

India's population of 1.1 billions is a positive as well as a negative factor just as it is in case of China. It is a very challenging task to raise the standard of living for the common man. It is a safe bet that the GDP figures will continue to rise along with per capita income. However, it seems an impossible task for these two countries to compare favorably with any of the Western European countries in terms of overall prosperity. Poverty, malnourishment, and ill health will continue to thrive there for the foreseeable future. After independence in 1947, the Indian Government had been following more or less an independent policy, leaning mostly towards left. However, 1991 brought a radical change; after the disintegration of USSR, India started moving towards the practice of the free economics. The result was phenomenal; the GNP started climbing at a rate of almost ten percent per year. Finally, India's economy took a positive turn.

INDIA'S MILITARY AND ECONOMIC STRENGTH

After sixty years of independence, India has become a global military power. It is a nuclear power. It has the fourth largest standing army, and its navy and air force are growing at a fast rate, though India still remains far behind China's military might. Just as with China, India has been buying weapons and military supplies from Russia. Things might change in future; the United States, Britain, France, and Israel are now leading competitors for the sales of military weapons. When it comes to military strength, India's vast population is a positive factor. Gradually, the Indian Government is moving forward towards modernization of its armed forces. Indians feel insecure with China and Pakistan and that is very true vice-versa .So a military build up and arms race has been emerging. All these three countries are spending billions of dollars to beef up their national security.

In the event of a nuclear war, no country would win. However, in a traditional war, it is difficult to predict who will win. China has defeated India in 1962 in a border dispute; India has defeated Pakistan twice, though Pakistan keeps the pressure on India. It is unfortunate that such resources are being spent on building military strength rather than on improving the conditions of the poor masses.

INDIA'S RELATIONS WITH OTHER COUNTRIES

India started as a nonaligned country as one of the founders of this group that still comprises about fifty countries worldwide. Recently, it has started moving towards the capitalistic system and the socialist approach is receding. The foreign policy of the Indian Government is still not aligned with any one nation; it is being dictated by the principle of national interests. Looking from a broad point of view, this may be the best way for an emerging country to carry itself. There is no dictating rationale that India should follow in the footsteps of the United States, or Russia, or any other country. We feel that China as well will not toe the line of Russia on the global stage and will not go against United States either. India and China will follow those policies that would be in the interest of their respective nations. They would avoid open confrontation with any global power unless there are some unforeseeable circumstances.

India's relations with Pakistan and China are not friendly; its relations with the United States, Russia, the United Kingdom, France, Japan and almost all other countries are normal and friendly. India can have good and influential relations with Sri Lanka, Bangladesh, the Philippines, Thailand, Indonesia, Nepal, and Vietnam if it takes appropriate steps towards these countries. In a decade or so, India will be in a good position to have a global voice in international affairs.

India started as a socialist country in 1947 when it gained its independence. And for forty years, until 1991, it followed the path of nurturing and sustaining heavily government-controlled public enterprises. The result was dismal. The government run industries took huge losses, and the country was not making any progress towards economic growth. In 1991, under the Prime Minister Narshim Rao and then Finance Minister Man Mohan Singh, began a free economy and a capitalistic, privately owned business model. It removed many restrictions that were imposed on the private industry before and provided incentives for private enterprise to move forward. The result was encouraging and the business sector started to move in the right direction. Back in 2004, Dr. Man Mohan Singh came into limelight and, at this time as the Prime Minister of India, he pushed further the role of free enterprise and private business.

This time, the Finance Minister was Mr. Chidambaran and he put the government machinery, fiscal policies, and its rules and regulations on track. India is going strong with a growth rate of 9 % in its yearly GNP. However, China is leading the world with a growth rate upwards of 10% or more. India's population is around 1.1 billion, second to China's which is 1.3 billion. The Gross National Income is around $2,000 per capita (2010 figures). The richest countries of the world, such as Sweden, have GNIs around $56,000 per capita. It shows how far the emerging countries like India, China and Brazil have to go. It is a long road

MILITARY SUPERIORITY

In terms of military might, India is behind the United States, Russia, and China. India is a nuclear power and it is upgrading its military arsenal gradually. Back in 1962, China had humbled India in its frontier territorial grab. Mr. Nehru, the Prime Minister of India at that time was shocked because the Chinese had made

Indians believe that they were brotherly nations and any kind of attack was just unimaginable. But such things do happen in the global arena. After 45 years, India and China are still talking and trying to resolve their differences. India and Pakistan, also a nuclear power now, have fought two wars over Kashmir. After sixty years, leaders of these two countries are still trying to find some solution. It seems that India is surrounded by two potential enemies, China in the East and Pakistan in the West.

Both China and Pakistan are ruled by dictators. Their militaries are solidly behind their leaders. Prime Minister Mrs. Gandhi pointed out in 1972 that India had to become a nuclear power because it was surrounded by two dangerous enemies. This situation still holds true because there is suspicion and mistrust between these nations. It will be a very scary scene if China and Pakistan together decide to act against India, considering that all the three countries are nuclear powers.

Anything is possible when leaders become power hungry. Political pundits will put their heads together and say with confidence that any move that might threaten the U.S. interests could be potentially dangerous. Before China really starts threatening the United States and its interests, it may try to ally with India and its growing military power. In a scenario like this, Russia would back up China and not India. We hope that none of these things will ever happen and the world will continue to be a safe place to live. The Indian leaders started with the principles of non-violence during the Gandhi era. Now, they realize that in the modern world it is just not possible. A country has to have a military deterrent for its survival.

POPULATION FACTORS

India's huge population is an economical problem for the government. To feed, to provide health, and education for such an enormous amount of people is indeed very challenging, especially when the country had seen abject poverty in the past centuries. It will take a very long time before an ordinary Indian citizen can live a life of reasonable comfort. The population growth has to be controlled either voluntarily or by law. In India, voluntary means are the only viable solutions. That will require lot of education and related health care for millions of people who live in Indian villages. It is not an easy task. The birth rates, as well as infant mortality rates, have to be controlled. Poverty and higher birth rates go hand in hand. A big family becomes a necessity for a poverty-stricken family's survival. The middle class is changing according to the norms of the modern times. However, it is the poor section of the society that is the major hurdle in fighting this problem. The population growth will continue in India, and its population may overtake the Chinese figures sooner rather than later.

WHERE INDIA WILL BE IN THE NEXT DECADE

Though the Indian economy is doing well, with a growth of about 9% in GNP per year since 2005, there is still a huge percentage of the population that is grinding under the conditions of severe poverty. These conditions will not change soon. It will require constant effort by the people and by the government to reverse this situation because it is on such a large scale. India needs a growth rate of ten percent every year for the next twenty or so years before poverty might be eradicated.

Every year, more and more people will join the middle class if the economy keeps up its growth rate. A lessening section of society will be facing the life and death questions of poverty. Unlike other countries, there will not be any civil unrest because of this situation. The main reason for this is the character of an Indian molded by patience, non-violence, and acceptance of the "Karma philosophy". It may not make any sense to those of a Western mindset, but this is the way it is in India.

MILITARY SUPERIORITY

As things stand today, India will continue to build a bigger and growingly modern military force. It has to build its own capabilities to defend itself and defend its allies. The same trend will be followed by the Chinese government. In other words, India and China may challenge the United States and Russia down the road for military supremacy. It seems that it may take two decades or so before this can come to fruition because the U.S. and Russia will also be upgrading their weapons and military arsenal in this same time frame. The constraints before the Indian and Chinese governments will be how to keep their population fed while progressing to this state of military advancement. It will be a big challenge. We can wish that every nation would give up nuclear bombs and missiles, and instead grow more wheat and corn in the fields, but that scenario is for another time and place that is still far away. The world will be moving towards more and more reasonable military deterrents. India will have to cope with the military pressure of China and Pakistan

RELATIONS WITH OTHER COUNTRIES

India and Pakistan

What will be the relationship between India and Pakistan during the next decade? It is difficult to say because there are lot of variables, uncertainties and if and buts questions. The number one factor is: dictatorship or a democratic government in Pakistan. The next consideration is the Chinese and Pakistani friendship. The third is socio-economical conditions in Pakistan. These three variables may dominate the relationship. Then there is a Kashmir problem. The

Kashmir problem is not easy to solve. Unless the people of India and Pakistan change their opinions and views drastically regarding the status of Kashmir, the governments of these countries will not be able to do anything.

We thus do not see any permanent solution in the next decade. One of the best solutions to the Kashmir issue could be similar to Canada's Quebec province, where the federal government has given the status to Quebec as a nation within Canada. If the Kashmiri people want to improve their standard of living, it will be in their own interest to realize the seriousness of this problem and give up terrorist activities for the dream of freedom; the Indian government will never agree to it. The government of Pakistan should be thinking in terms of fair autonomy for the people of Kashmir state and nothing more. This way of thinking might pave a solution to this intricate problem.

The next ten years could forge good neighborly relations provided both countries emphasize the importance of business relations rather than a solution to the Kashmir issue. As it appears now, the Pakistani government will continue to harp on the Kashmir issue. The Pakistani Taliban group, as well as other anti-India Islamist groups will be a constant threat to Indian security. India-Pakistani relations do not show signs of moving towards a collaborative environment.

India and China

In the next decade, there are several foreseeable scenarios. The first scenario is that India and China may follow a path towards mutually friendly relations. They might compete in all fields while still maintaining close relations. The second scenario is the possibility that India leans towards the interests of the United States to counterbalance the influence of China and Russia. Another possibility is that China and Pakistan forge a military pact against India. It is certain that India and China are going to play important roles in the global political arena in the coming decade.

The last sixty years are bound to play an important part in shaping the future policies of India, China and Pakistan. If the governments and the people of these countries forget the misunderstanding and mistrust that prevails strongly in these countries against each other, then there are good chances that these countries follow the first, more positive scenario. The second scenario holds very important possibilities. There are about two million Indians living in the United States. They have assimilated well and enjoyed economic success in the United States mainstream.

This section of Indians, living in the United States along with the general public in India, favors the United States more than any other country. This is the present assessment. It may or may not change in the next ten years. It all depends upon personal relations between the national leaders of these countries that dictate the policies of the governments.

There are good possibilities that India and the United States become closer as times move forward. The credit for this must be given to President Bill Clinton and President George W. Bush and Prime Minister Man Mohan Singh should this scenario becomes a reality. It does not exclude the possibility that India and China still maintain good relations. Similarly, it does not insure that they do not become active adversaries. Chinese and Indians know it very well that any future war will not produce any winner or loser and that the boundary line dispute will linger on. However, the trade and business deals should and will increase between these growing nations. Indo-Chinese relations are at cross roads.

India and Russia

Before the disintegration of the USSR and the demise of the communism in 1991, India and Russia had built friendly and close relationship between them. The socialist India was relying heavily on the system of public enterprise and was partially closed to the free market system. After the breakdown of Russian empire, the government of India started thinking in terms of private enterprise and a free economy. The meltdown of the Russian economy in 1998 reinforced the changes in Indian economic and fiscal policies. President Boris Yeltsin and Vladimir Putin were not overwhelmingly concerned with India, a stark contrast to the past relations that were very cozy. The Russian government had supported India in the Kashmir dispute with Pakistan. Most of the military weaponry was bought from Russia, something that continues today. What factors are going to affect the relations between India and Russia in the next decade? There are two. If India moves towards the United States more closely, there might be some repercussion. At the very least, the existing relations would become somewhat disjointed. Secondly, if China and India enter some kind of conflict, the chances are that the Russian government may take a neutral stand or side with China.

We should consider language and cultural differences, as well as the role played by the local population too. There are few Indians living in Russia, whereas two million Indians live in the United States, sharing English as the common language of communication. These two factors indicate that there are stronger chances for India and the United States to become closer in the next ten years than India and Russia. This factor is only an assumption and it may not prove true. It does not mean that trade and business relations will be adversely effected. India needs oil and gas and Russia can supply both of these commodities.

We feel that the relations between India and Russia will continue to move in a positive direction. In the past, Russia had been a good friend of India and it seems that this will continue. Very recently, in March of 2010, Russian Prime Minister Putin signed a pact with India to build more than ten nuclear reactors to generate electric power, a deal that is worth billions of dollars.

India and Japan

Relations between India and Japan will continue to be friendly in the coming decade. Japan's Prime Minister Abe has told the Prime Minister Man Mohan

Singh that a sizeable amount of investment will be made by Japanese companies in India. Presently, Indo –Japanese trade plays a role of lesser significance. Indian I.T companies have not been able to secure any big business deals in Japan so far. Suzuki and Honda are doing well in India. However, South Korean companies like Hyundai, LG, and others have built big manufacturing facilities in India. As far as political relations are concerned, the strategic policies of the United States with India and China will have important connotation regarding Indo- Japanese friendship. In East Asia, Japan and Australia are the two most reliable allies of the United States. Japanese foreign policy reflects this connection. Exciting relations between countries are built on certain criteria. Language, culture, religion, past historical interactions and number of people living presently from the other country are important factors that lay down solid foundations for a flourishing relationship. The trade statistic is important, but not vital to such relationships. India and Japan could become closer allies in a case where China starts its aggressive posturing in Southeast Asia.

India and Canada

Countries are just like big communities; interactions between individuals and groups of people within the community shape the mold. With a greater understanding between the people of these different groups and individuals comes the greater chance for a good rapport amongst them. Canada has almost three million Canadians of Indian origin. It is a binding force between India and Canada. Western Canada has a large population of Indian farmers. However, the recent migration of Indians is based in the province of Ontario, the most industrialized region of Canada.

The population of Canadian Indians is a mix of highly educated and skilled people with people of lower skills and lesser education. Unlike the United States, not all belong to the elite group of the Canadian society. Whereas Indian Americans are highly skilled, educated, and professional group of people, the Canadian Indians do not always fall into similar classifications. Indian Americans have established themselves very well in the business sector, as well as in the government. If the conditions of Canadian Indians become similar to the Indian Americans, things will become very different. Right now, there are pockets of unequal opportunities for many Indians and Asian communities alike. There is hope this will change when the Indian community picks up important positions in the Canadian socio-economical hierarchy. The government agencies would thus then begin to change their positions; opening up and integrating Indians into mainstream Canada. We hope that in the next ten years, the Canadian Indian community will move up fast and steadily. This would surely have a very positive impact on the relations between India and Canada.

When this milestone is achieved, the very next move from this community would be to invest in India. That builds up bridges of greater cooperation and friendship between the two countries. The role of the personalities of national leaders always plays a significant part in bringing national friendships to the higher levels. When we factor these considerations in our assessment of future relations between India and Canada, we feel that these relations will grow to maturity and greater potentialities within the next ten years. We do not see any reason why they would not be better, and that is our hope.

India, France, Germany and the European Union

India has normal and friendly relations with France, Germany and the E.U. It is nothing spectacular; there are no big disputes or issues that might harm the relationship. India had been trying to get more investment from E.U. countries but has not been successful so far. There are very few companies of French and German origin who run businesses in Indian market. Trade is minimal. Very few Indians live in France and Germany. The overall picture is that these relations are more or less formal. There is nothing substantial in these relationships, whether culturally, socially, or monetarily. The next ten years do not indicate any big changes from the current position. The E.U. will likely put greater investment in Eastern European countries rather than in the developing countries of Asia or Latin America, primarily because of the location and common heritage. As the Eastern European countries attain higher standard of living, the E.U. would divert its attention to Asia and South America. The Indian I.T. industry might help in creating favorable conditions to build closer relations at least in terms of business partnership. The language barrier is a big hurdle. The leaders of these countries did not show a keen interest in nurturing closer ties, as demonstrated by the past.

India, Mexico and Brazil

Ten years from now where will these countries be economically, socially, and politically? Let us examine each country. Mexico presently has a population of 110 million strong, and a GNI around $7,000 per capita. Mexico exports crude oil to the United States. The country has a very rich cultural history going back to the Mayans. Negatively speaking, Mexico has been plagued by drug cartels. It is a poor country; there is a big divide between the rich and the poor people. The result is that there has been a big migration of Mexican people to the United States.

Though Mexico is a founding member of N.A.F.T.A., it has failed to make a big difference in the socio-economical life of the ordinary Mexican citizen. Unless United States and the other industrialized countries of Europe invest heavily in Mexico, and if the Mexican government helps the growth of industry, there is a strong likelihood that the next ten years will not change much. Mexico will move forward economically, but it will be at a slow pace. We do not anticipate a growth rate of 8-10 % in the GNP. The Mexican labor class will continue to migrate to the United States, legally or illegally. Mexico is not a military power and therefore does not carry any clout in the foreign affairs of the globe. However, it is a democratic country and is non-communist. It can exert a powerful influence over other South American countries.

Brazil is the largest South American country. It has a population of 190 million people of different origins. The GNI is $8,000 per capita. It is self-sufficient in energy resources and rich in iron ore. It has, very recently, become the largest manufacturer of ethanol. Like Mexico, there is a big divide between the rich and poor. There is a large and growing gap between the urban upper middle class family and that of the rural farmer.

The past President of Brazil, Mr. Lula, was trying his best to narrow this glaring difference in the standard of living. Like other South American countries, Brazil needs a well educated, business oriented, and enterprising youth movement to take the country forward through hard work and determination. The country is full of natural resources, but social disparities have to be removed. Dynamic leadership can take the country to such desired heights.

How the next ten years are going to shape Brazil is dependent upon many factors. It all depends on courageous leadership of the country to make things happen, by bringing more investment money and setting up world class organizations. Brazil, like Mexico, is not a military power, but being the largest South American country it has global influence in the political sphere. Many leaders of the country have a leftist leaning and are not sold on capitalism to solve the economic problems facing the country.

How is India going to forge its relations in the next ten years with these two countries? Most probably, it will be friendly, cordial, and progressive- along such lines. The government would like to increase its business relations in terms of more import and export. More cultural exchanges are possible. India might offer training in technical areas like information technology and other fields. It is interesting to note that India, Brazil and South Africa have formed a close knitted group to foster greater trade amongst them as well as to take a common political approach in international politics.

India and Australia

Sixty years ago, Australia practiced "White Only" policies. Asians were not allowed to settle down in Australia. Things have since changed. Thousand of Indian students are enrolled in Australian universities now. In fact, many Indians now prefer to go to Australia rather than England or the U.S. because it is closer and less expensive. The present relationship between India and Australia is formal and not very close. Trade and business connections are not booming. With the present prevailing conditions in Europe, the potential migrant worker from Eastern Europe would rather stay in Europe and not move to Australia. That opens the door more widely for Asians, especially Indians and Chinese, to fill this labor gap.

There is no doubt that Australian economy will continue to advance in the next ten years; the GNI presently, is around $43,000 per capita ; will likely to increase. Since India has the advantage of speaking English and has enjoyed close connections with England, it would not be difficult for Indians to assimilate into Australian society. Since the present migration of Indians mainly consists of highly educated and technical personnel, they will establish themselves very well in the Australian professional group.

These are important factors when we consider the future relations between India and Australia. It will be mutually beneficial for India and Australia to establish closer ties in terms of business, as well as social and political connections. The future leaders of India and Australia can make it happen because good foundations have now been laid. It is generally true that the relations between countries are governed by the degree of interactions, social and economical, between the locals and the migrant community. The new comers have to adapt themselves to mingle smoothly into the fabric of local society. This happens when the new community has established itself well, economically. If Australia wants to become a global power, it has to increase immigration and should be ready to accept Asians with open arms and without any reservation. Twenty million people, the present population of Australia, must continue to grow to exert a global influence. Without it, Australia would likely be like any other Western European nation with no military power and with no global influence.

Very recently, in January 2010, many Indian students were attacked in Melbourne. The Australian government denounced it. At one point, it became a very tense situation. The relations between India and Australia took a nasty hit. It is hoped that this serious situation will be handled appropriately by the Australian government.

India and Korea

South Korea is an example of a shining star state; it has transformed itself into a highly industrialized and technically advanced country. The present GNI is $18,000 per capita; the population is 50 million people. Companies like Hyundai, Samsung, LG, and others have become global corporations. The present trade between South Korea and India is higher than Indo-Japanese business. The President of South Korea paid a visit to India in January of 2010 and signed some significant business deals. Included in this was the setting up of a nuclear reactor for generating electrical power. South Korean companies are world class and close business relations between Indian and South Korean companies will prove to be beneficial. The government of India should provide attractive incentives to the Korean companies to invest in India. We see increased trading partnership with South Korea continuing in the next decade. There are no political issues or any other socio-economical areas of disagreement between these two countries. There is no reason why these business relations cannot continue and expand in the next decade.

India and England

India and England have a long history of relations on the international stage. Interestingly, independent India selected a royal British citizen, Lord Mountbatten, as its first Governor General. Most of the top Indian leaders, from Gandhi, to Nehru, to Radhakrishnan, attended famous colleges and universities in England. The British Labor Party, headed by Mr. Attle, was instrumental in advancing the cause of Indian freedom. The first Prime Minister of India, Mr. Nehru, tried to follow the same kind of socialist policies that were in place in England at that time.

In 1989, India was entrenched in socialism and the country was going nowhere. The relations between India and England were not very warm- they were cordial. During the last five years or so, from 2005 forward, the bilateral relations between these two countries have become close. The present Prime Minister of India, Dr. Man Mohan Singh, and former Prime Minister Tony Blair have brought India and England closer than ever before. There are more than one million Indians living in Great Britain and they are enjoying all the benefits that this great country can provide to its citizens. The trade between these two countries is growing. The English language has forged a common link between English and Indian people. Indian food is popular in England, especially in London. Indians are starting new businesses. London has become an open door for Indian companies to go through to other European markets. It seems likely that India and England will follow close, friendly relations, growing from those that are in place today.

India and the Muslim World

These days, terrorists and so called Jihadists are prominent in the news media all over the world. A very small extremist group of people have created feelings of fear and danger for the general public. We do not know when a suicide bomber will decide to kill himself along with other people. It is very unfortunate that these young people have given up on the hopes and dreams that could change their lives and their beliefs. Our efforts should be to provide all channels of help to them in terms of monetary support and proper educational guidance. Their brains have been tainted with false propaganda, lies, and empathy. If we could undo that without resorting to guns and grenades, that would be wonderful. Somehow, things are not currently progressing in the right directions. Probably it will have to be Muslim religious leaders, along with government and private institutions, who can change this situation. If this group of extreme-minded people is not brought into mainstream, the world will be exposed, plagued with untold misery and sorrow. As things stand today, the solution of bombs and firepower is going nowhere. If the hardcore extremists do not change their views, then the only course left for the governments is to exterminate the group. It will be painful and undesirable, but perhaps the only viable course of action left to get rid of the problem.

India has a very large population of Muslims - almost 150 million. The largest Muslim country in terms of population is Indonesia with a population of 230 millions. So for India the Muslim community, though a small minority of about ten percent of the population, carry a significant political, social, and economical importance. Luckily, India is almost free of these suicide attacks when compared to Iraq, Pakistan, Afghanistan, and Palestine. The government of India naturally has to be very sensitive and careful about this issue. Like any other country, India has to lay out its foreign policy strategically regarding other Muslim countries. Let us start with neighboring Bangladesh.

India and Bangladesh

With the help of Indian army, Bangladesh was created in 1971. Pakistan was badly defeated and it lost the province of East Bengal, which became Bangladesh. Almost three decades have gone by and Bangladesh is still among the poorest countries in the world. The leadership is still groping in darkness and is not effective. The future remains bleak unless some dynamic political figure emerges and changes its fortunes. The government of India should help Bangladesh in terms of financial aid and other infrastructural support. It is to India's own advantage to have Bangladesh as an independent nation that is favorably inclined towards India rather than to China or Pakistan. The investment in Bangladesh will be beneficial to India. Unlike Pakistan, which keeps up animosity towards India without cessation, Bangladesh could ultimately be a good ally for India. West Bengal, an Indian state, has almost every thing in common with Bangladesh except the religion. These two regions can forge good, friendly relations. The chance of any kind of skirmish or threat of aggression against one another is minimal.

India and Afghanistan

Historically, India and Afghanistan have maintained a non-hostile and even friendly relationship during the time when Afghanistan was ruled by the monarchy. Then, the monarchy was overthrown and the Russians came along, attempting to spread communism. It did not work; the local population hated the Russians. Then Pakistan and the United States created the Taliban. In 1989, the Russians were forced out. The United States abandoned the nation after the Russians withdrawal, leaving the country in the hands of Taliban. The local warlords, with the help of Taliban rule, became the authority of Afghanistan. The country went backward to Sharia's laws and the fate of women was sealed. It became worse than Khoemeni's Iran. President George W. Bush, in 2001, went after Al Qaeda and an American army invaded Afghanistan. Interestingly, at this time, the Americans were fighting against the Taliban because Al Qaeda and Taliban were the new rulers of the nation. The present condition is that Al Qaeda and Taliban are well entrenched on the borders of Pakistan and the government of President Karzai does not have the support of the local people.

He can not stay in his position without the help of the United States and other Western nations.

President Karzai is friendly towards India - he had studied in India – and has built up a good rapport with Prime Minister Man Mohan Singh. Without Karzai, can India maintain good relations with Afghanistan? Or would it even like to? As things stand today, Afghanistan could become problematic for the American administration and other Western powers. India does not have the necessary resources to build its friendship with Afghanistan. Also, it does not have any power to fight against Al Qaeda and Taliban. As time progresses, India might just leave Afghanistan to its own fate, take a neutral position as the country rebuilds. It has become difficult to form any concrete policy due to the fluid and changing nature of Afghanistan.

Right now Pakistan feels that India has taken an upper hand and it has taken a back seat in terms of its relations with Afghanistan. This is not acceptable to the Pakistani government. Afghanistan remains a puzzling state under the present conditions.

India and Pakistan

Back in 1947, when Pakistan came into existence after the British government decided to partition India into two separate states, more than a million people died during this transition. India and Pakistan waged two wars; wars that have damaged the relations between these two countries to this day and exists as nothing but cold and unfriendly. For more than sixty years, the problem of Kashmir has separated these two countries. This situation is somewhat similar to Tibet or Quebec.

Unless and until the general public of the two countries agree to a solution, the leaders of either country will not be able to impose their plans. There is no national leader in both of these countries that can command respect of the general public through this very serious situation. It seems that India and Pakistan will keep up talks for some time until the general public of both these countries agree to a solution. Only then can these two countries live in peace.

The Pakistani government will likely keep up the pressure on India to come up with some solution; however, nothing substantial is going to happen. Indian leaders have no choice; the days of Nehru and Gandhi have gone. There is no leader of that caliber who could resolve this on their own. The momentum of the public voice is very crucial at this current juncture.

India and Indonesia

India and Indonesia got their freedom from their colonial masters almost at the same time in 1947. India's then Prime Minister, Mr. Nehru, and Indonesian President Mr. Sukarno were good friends. India and Indonesia laid out "Panch Sheel," five principles to propagate the non-alignment movement of the developing world. More than fifty countries were active members of this group at one time. When President Sukarno was removed by General Suharto, the cordial and close relations between India and Indonesia were broken. Indonesia was ruled by a military dictator; the political scenery had changed. India was still a democratic country and the leaders of both countries drifted apart. In many ways, India was ahead of Indonesia in terms of good governance and having an educated middle class.

Going back further in history, Indonesia has had very close cultural and religious affinities with India. Buddhism and Hinduism were the driving force of Indonesian society in sixth and seventh centuries A.D. By the 12th century, Indonesia had embraced the Muslim religion. However, Bali, a small island of Indonesia, is still a Hindu kingdom. The people of Indonesia practice a moderate Muslim religion and are not very orthodox in their followings, unlike Iran and Saudi Arabia. Presently, Indonesia has a democratically elected government. The country is making fairly decent progress towards industrial growth.

India can help Indonesia in many ways, whether it is through direct foreign investment or other means. Indonesia has established good commercial relations with Malaysia and China. The Chinese-Indonesian community can make some important contributions in these regards. They have the experience and connections with outside Chinese businesses. The present indications of Indonesian government show that Malaysia and China will continue to be the prominent trading partners of Indonesia. We do not see any great eagerness on the part of Indian industry to enter the Indonesian markets. India and Indonesia will likely maintain good and friendly relations.

India and Malaysia

Malaysia got its independence in 1957. During the British regime, many Indians, mostly the labor class had migrated to Malaysia to work on the rubber plantations. After independence, the Malaysian government set up legal policy of promoting only the local Malay people, known as Boom Putras or sons of the soil, for higher government and public offices and therefore depriving Indians and Chinese the chance to move up in the Malaysian hierarchy. The Chinese, at about 30% of the population, have established themselves well in the business sector, the 10% Indian population is still toiling in the labor market, and the 60% Bhoomi-Putras are occupying all the governmental positions.

Malaysia has a good reserve of oil and gas. In addition, many foreign companies have set up electronic manufacturing bases. The present and the past governments have a strong leaning towards Muslim culture. Hindus and Christians have seen visible discriminations in this society. The position of Indians remains at the bottom layer .The Indian community has to do something to come out of this pitiable situation; if the Malay government does something, the picture would certainly change. Yet, it looks like the government is not going to do anything drastic to change this position. The Indian government has to put some pressure on the Malaysian government to improve the plight of local Indians.

India and Iran

The foreign policy of any country is dictated by many considerations. Trade relations, cultural interactions, mutual respect and appreciation, historical links, and future prospects are all entities that have to be examined closely before proceeding with any important international relationship. Iran has lots of gas and oil resources. Indian industry needs a large chunk of it. Thus, there is a need for business ties. The present regime of Iran is run by Muslim clerics. It is trying to become a nuclear power. Many people consider Iran a dangerous country. Would India gain anything from the present leadership of Iran? The answer is a simple no. Iranian society has gone backward by at least twenty five years. It would be better off for India to keep Iran at a distance. Business has to proceed, but other things have to wait. Iranian government, however, would like to establish good relations with India because it stands to gain many things. What about the social and cultural ties with Iran? It will be better to wait till the main stream of Iranian society give up the old, silly, and stupid religious dogmas set up by Muslim clerics.

India and Iraq

Iraq will take a long time before it becomes a stable nation. Like Iran, Iraq is rich with oil and gas, and India will have to do business with it sooner or later. In the past, there existed no close relations with India and Iraq. We do not see India establishing closer ties with it in the near future. Unlike the United Arab Countries (U.A.E), not many workers came to Iraq to work from India. Historically there are no links between these two countries. It will be decades before Iraq will be able to support itself both monetarily and culturally.

India and Saudi Arabia

Saudi Arabia is a conservative, orthodox and highly religious country. It has the largest reserve of oil and gas and therefore commands respect in international affairs. However, the country is not a military power. It can defend itself, but not others. The chief of Al Qaeda, Bin Laden happens to be a prince of Saudi Arabia. The Saudis monarchy promotes Muslim religion throughout the world. It is a country of wealth, as well of extreme poverty. Women are not held equal to men in their society. It is a country of very outdated norms and traditions. Mecca and Medina are located in Saudi Arabia where millions of Muslims go for performing Haj. Since there is no animosity between the people of India and Saudi-Arabia, friendly relations between these two countries will continue to be the norm.

INDIA AND EGYPT

India and Egypt were the founding members of the non-alignment group. Nehru, India's Prime Minister and Nasser, the Egyptian President were good friends. As President Sadat came into power, Egypt had moved out of Russian influence and became closer to the United States. India remained a staunch ally of Russia. Nehru, a Socialist, was not close to the capitalist United States. India and Egypt drifted in different directions and the old emotional attachment had evaporated as time progressed. Presently, India and Egypt have normal and friendly ties, but nothing beyond that. Egypt and India could once again establish closer relations for their mutual good. Egypt is a progressive, modern country that could play important role in molding 21st century values upon young Muslim men and women. Egypt could follow the footsteps of Turkey in transforming the extremist, religious thinking of the general public to a secular base. The Muslim world needs this direction.

CHAPTER 5

China

How a poor agricultural Asian country could transform itself into the world's manufacturing workshop is an amazing story. In just three decades, China uplifted millions of its citizens from poverty to prosperity. This progress has continued, reaching higher and higher heights. With a 10% annual rate of growth in its GDP, China ranks as the third largest economy of the world. The way China is moving forward, there is no surprise that it could surpass Japan and might come very close to rivaling the strength of the United States economy. Only time will tell us if this will happen.

CHINA'S ECONOMIC STRENGTH

At this juncture, China's manufacturing structure is geared towards basic consumer goods. It is not highly sophisticated and technical, unlike Japan's and Germany's manufacturing industry. The most important trading partners of China at this time are Japan, the United States, the European Union, South Korea, and Russia. China has the advantage of a huge population base with low wages, and that will be a very difficult factor for American or European countries to compete with China in terms of pricing. Its industrial structure supports pragmatic opportunities. However, it does not have a well defined legal system and business rules and regulations are not followed. The Communist Party plays a dominant role in enforcing the laws.

The communist government of China is highly capitalistic in nature and it manages the industrial production smoothly and efficiently; the country is moving forward at a rapid pace. There is lot of corruption at the government level, but things are being done fairly well. Production keeps up the necessary pace for such exponential growth. Products made in China are available throughout the world. Presently, it is an export oriented economy with minimal internal consumption. This is a big difference between U.S economy and that of China. If the Chinese government is able to guide the industrial policy in the way it has done in the past decades, there is a very good chance that the Chinese economy will continue to advance at a phenomenal rate, and, in a short period of time, it will surpass Japan to become the second biggest economy of the world.

RELATIONS OF CHINA WITH OTHER COUNTRIES

It is very clear that there will be no individual power that will dominate the events of the world. Ten years down the road, we see at least five emerging countries that will have a large say in what goes on in our world. The leading most country will continue to be the United States; the European Union with NATO will also emerge as a powerful force. China, Russia, India, and Brazil are also emerging as players in this power game. Among the emerging countries, China will take the lead, though it is true Russia is more powerful in terms of military strength compared to China. However, it seems Russia will not be able to match the Chinese business strength.

Most of the Chinese military armaments come from Russia, but China is building its military strength indigenously, now. China would like to maintain good relations with the United States, being its biggest trading partner and having billions invested in U.S. Treasuries. Additionally, there are almost two millions Chinese living in the United States. Thus, China will not deliberately take a clashing course against the United States unless its own survival and other compelling reasons come into play. China will not likely challenge Russia either. It seems unlikely at this juncture that it will engage into a full-fledged war with India, though it keeps up the pressure on India with the boundary dispute. Most likely, China will follow its own independent foreign policy that will be governed by its national interests. It will not toe the Russian line and it will try to improve its relations with Japan.

CHINA TEN YEARS FROM NOW

The present China has 1.3 billion people, $ 3300, GNI per capita, a growth rate exceeding ten percent in GNP, and is a nuclear power. They will dominate the global arena in the coming ten years. It is the only communist country that has become a highly efficient capitalistic society. The government is run by the Communist Party hierarchy. The ordinary citizen does not have the freedom of speech, freedom of religion, or other human rights. But the country is booming; in fact, it has become the manufacturing center of the world. With the present rate of growth, it might take the second place replacing Japan as the most dynamic economy in the world.

The zest and the skill sets of the present generation will move China further ahead, both economically and politically. We can assume that when China makes such strides that the ordinary citizen might have more freedom of expression, including the freedom to criticize the communist leadership, freedom to follow any religion, and freedom to be free from government pressure. This is only an assumption; it may or may not happen. We can go back to communist regime of Russia and analyze what happened during Stalin's dictatorship.

The Chinese people have paid a very heavy price to Chairman Mao's policies. They have lost all their freedoms. All the material gains can not replace the freedom of soul. There is no doubt that millions of Chinese have come out of poverty and hundreds of them have become millionaires. The chances are that this trend will continue to move forward, yet we should not forget that such a huge population of 1.3 billions will take a long time to transform itself to be called a rich country. It will take decades to reach to a level of a GNI of $43,000 per capita, which is the present average figure for the rich Western countries.

MILITARY SUPERIORITY

With the help of formerly communist Russia, China has built a formidable military army. The present government of China will not follow a policy of non-aggression or peaceful negotiations with other countries if it sees that the other country is vulnerable or weak. It seems that the present leadership of China believes in the principle of strength, and thus it would be advisable for its neighbors to guard itself against possible confrontation with China. Russia and India had seen this manifestation in the events of the past.

Since India is also a nuclear power, the Chinese government might think that the United States and India may form a military and political alliance between them to counterbalance the Chinese influence in the Pacific and South Asia. Depending upon the prevailing situation and circumstances, this kind of alliance between the U.S. and India is highly possible. If the Chinese leadership maintains a peaceful posture towards India regarding the disputed territories, then there are equally high chances that both countries may keep progressing as non-aligned national powers. In any dispute with China, Russia may take a neutral position or favor China, just as the United States would most likely side with India. Pakistan is bound to go with China under those conditions. During the next ten years, China and India will continue to build their military strengths and may very well maintain peaceful and friendly relations. The ball will be in the Chinese court. We can predict with good probability that India will not take the first step against China; however, based upon past history, Chinese leaders might venture out aggressively again. It looks likely that China would have a bigger influence in East Asia than India

RELATIONS WITH OTHER COUNTRIES

China and the United States

The new President of the United States, Mr. Obama, seems very eager to establish closer relations with China, a stark contrast to when Mr. Bush was the President. China was not openly hostile to the United States; yet, the Chinese government was creating problems in a round about way for the United States.

The American government was playing a similar game, raising issues of human rights violations, supporting the Tibetan cause, encouraging Dali Lama, and standing firm with the Taiwanese Government. The Chinese have declared openly that Taiwan is an integral part of China and it can not be considered an independent country. The leaders of Taiwan sometimes support the independence and sometime want to merge with China.

The present government of Taiwan is establishing closer ties with the Republic of China; whether the general public wants it or not is difficult to predict. In the past, the U.S. government assured Taiwan that it will support the independent state of Taiwan. China does not seem willing to wage an open war against the U.S. over the issue of Taiwan. However, if the future government of Taiwan does declare its independence, there exists the possibility for serious skirmishes and possible military clashes.

The present economical conditions do not dictate any of these scenarios taking place as China has invested billions of its dollars in the U.S treasury bonds. Secondly, China cannot afford to lose its business with the United States and other Western countries. Taiwan and China will maintain a status quo position for a long time to come. Relations with the United States will be based upon the realities that China will be a strong competitor against the United States in many aspects of global policies, both regionally and internationally. President Obama realizes the importance of China based upon trade and business factors with the United States. Nobody would advise to lose the advantages that the United States has in maintaining friendly relations with China.

Future Assessment

The Chinese economy will continue to grow by 8-10% every year and that will mean it is going to become the second largest economy in the world, replacing Japan. It would be really tricky to get the number one slot, as the United States will probably remain the biggest economical power in the world. With trillions of dollars in foreign reserve funds, China will continue to expand its military might. However, it will not be able to match the mighty power of the United States or that of Russia. These two superpowers will continue to be number one and number two. It can thus be safe to assume that China will avoid conflict with these two major players. The major problem area is Taiwan. Will the United States enter an open war against China on this issue? It is difficult to say. The United States surely will help Taiwan, but to what extent and how has yet to be seen.

The United States wants help from China to bring North Korea to the negotiating table in stopping its nuclear activities. China has friendly relations with North Korea and the Western world thinks that China can help. So far the results have not been successful. The United States also want China to do away with its repressive policies towards freedom of speech, freedom to worship, and other human rights. Here too, there is very little progress. China has created an amazingly successful capitalistic society but it still runs on rigid and firm communist rules and regulations. It will take some time for that freedom to emerge.

China and North Korea

It was the Chinese army that had fought against the American forces back in 1950 on the Korean peninsula. The country was divided into North and South, and ever since that time North Korea has remained a good friend of China. These two countries are still close to each other; however, the recent years show the lessening of Chinese influences over North Korea. The present dictator of North Korea wants to become a nuclear power.

The United Nations has given many warnings to North Korea not to proceed with its nuclear plan, but the North Korean government had just ignored it. Countries like the United States, Japan, China, Russia and South Korea have put their pressure on North Korea, but it did not work. Though North Korea and China have been allies for decades, they could do nothing about this matter.

Though the country is undergoing extreme and harsh conditions such as poverty, hunger, and unemployment, there still there has been no positive response from North Korea. The government of South Korea had promised all kinds of help for the people of North Korea, but the dictator does not want to listen. That shows that China, South Korea, and Japan have no or very little influence on North Korea. It wants substantial economic aid from the United States and from other countries. Just like Iran, North Korea has become a hot spot in the global political arena.

Future Directions

The best thing that Chinese leadership can do to help poor North Korea is to convince its leaders, Kim Jong and his group, to abandon the idea of becoming a nuclear state. Instead of wasting all the money on this activity, it would be much better to spend the money on education, health care, and agricultural production. Then at least the people would not be starving and the whole country would be better off. South Korea and China can set up manufacturing facilities there; creating jobs and improving the standard of living for the average citizen.

North Korean leaders should realize that they may not be able to get American help; they should invite South Korean, Chinese, and Japanese companies to invest in their country. It is irony that dictators all over the world create a lot of hardship and misery for a common man. It is very true in the case of Kim Jong and company. The notion that the United States will provide financial aid in the case of North Korea so that they abandon their nuclear ambitions may work out.

The most reliable source for uplifting the North Korean economy is South Korea. Next is China and then Japan. At present, the Chinese companies are busy setting up manufacturing plants in their own country, but down the road they will start looking for foreign locations where the cost of production will be lower than their own country. North Korea is bound to get attention from the Chinese corporate executives. It will be mutually advantageous for China and North Korea.

China

If the North Korean leaders do not stop their nuclear ambition, it would be most unfortunate for the Korean people. The Chinese government should use their good relations to reverse this process. An international plan supported by the United States, Russia, Japan, China and Western countries, along with financial aid from agencies like the IMF and the Asian Development Bank may be the best future directions for North Korea and its people.

China and Pakistan

China and Pakistan have established very friendly relations between them. President Musharaff of Pakistan and President Hu of China are instrumental in charting out these relations. Back in the 50's, China and India, both founders of the non-alignment movement, were very close. The China attack on India in 1962, which was very shocking to India, left all the built in reservoir of friendship destroyed. Pakistan waged war against India in 1948 and again in 1965 over Kashmir. China backed Pakistan whereas India was supported by Russia. The leadership of Pakistan wanted the friendship of China as a counterbalance against India.

China too considers friendship with Pakistan as a counterbalance against India. Pakistan and China are united because they see India as a common enemy. The Kashmir problem between India and Pakistan will take a long time to resolve. The border problem between India and China also seems very difficult to solve logistically. Keeping this background in mind, it could be predicted that relations between China and Pakistan will continue to move forward. Relations between China, Pakistan and India will move very gradually towards normalcy, unless China and Pakistan change their present positions.

There are many factors that will prevent establishing friendly relations between these countries. The next decade does not show any dramatic sign of improved relations between India and China and Pakistan. Historically, the Chinese and Pakistani governments are aggressive in their territorial policies, while the general atmosphere in India is not favorable to Pakistan and China. It will take a long time to change

Future Directions

Pakistan and China will continue to be good and reliable friends. Both countries need each other. Pakistan leaders might start some kind of mini war against India on the grounds of the Kashmir issue to appease their anti India groups, but a major conflict is not foreseeable because it is the worldly consensus that wars do not solve any problems, but only aggravates the situation.

China and India will not go to war over border disputes. China will continue to occupy the Indian territory and India would continue to raise its opposition. These situations look bleak.

China and the E.U

China has taken a dynamic place in manufacturing arena. China will continue to export ready made garments and basic manufactured products to the E.U. at cheaper prices and in huge quantities. The E.U. has had to restrict this influx in the past. It will take sometime for China to compete against highly industrialized Western countries for sophisticated and highly technical engineering products. It can be assumed that China will take a back seat in Europe as far as establishing manufacturing plants are concerned.

China, Iran, Saudi Arabia and Middle Eastern Countries

China is looking to all corners of the world to get oil and gas to satisfy its booming industry. There is no other reason than this for the establishment of good commercial relations between China and Iran, Saudi Arabia, the U.A.E. and others. Presently, Iraq is not a possible partner. At the same time, China is looking for more markets for its products. Most of these Middle Eastern countries are very religious and China is communist. Religion does not play any role in government policies in China. Thus, there are no common socio-cultural and religious threads. As it seems now, China is going to take a very powerful position in the world. The Middle Eastern countries will likely try to establish friendly commercial relations with China. In the long run, China could become a good source for investment in these countries. However, like Japan, China will concentrate its investment in Southeast Asia.

China and Russia

These two giant countries are still friends though Russia has renounced communism. After the death of Stalin, Mao-Zedong declared that he would be the one who would direct the movement of communism in the world and rightly so, as China is now the most powerful communist country in the world. China and Russia collaborated with each other in spreading communism to other countries, like North Korea, Vietnam, and Cambodia in the past.

Russia is the biggest supplier of military equipment and armaments to China. The trade relations between these two countries are on the rise. China has obtained exploratory rights for gas and oil in Russian oil fields.

Like Russia, China is a nuclear power and has one of the largest military forces. As time goes by, Russia will be stronger economically and would like to regain its place as a superpower. China would like to follow this lead. In this context, Japan would like to change its military policy. If the United States agrees, Japan could become a nuclear power. The relations between Russia and China seem to be going smoothly and we do not see any immediate danger of disruption.

How Russia would react if India and China should engage each other in some kind of conflict is a difficult thing to predict. Since India and Russia are also good friends, Russia would probably assume a peacemaking role. It can not afford to be anti-China. We feel Russia and China would follow their independent policies as well as collaborate with each other in foreign policy matters. The United States will be skeptical and cautious with both of these countries.

Future Projections

China and Russia will be close allies in future too. China will continue to build its military might and Russia will be a big supplier, not only of arms, but of oil and gas too. In the case of any future conflict with Taiwan, Russia would support China. However, if there is any conflict with India, Russia may just remain neutral. It does not seem likely that they would go against India. Russia does not have an ambition to have big influence in the Southeastern Asian countries like Cambodia, Laos, and Vietnam, whereas China would like to have its say and exert its presence. China will expand its investments in the areas of oil and gas in Russia and, down the road, in other areas of manufacturing as well. Russian companies might think of putting some money in China also, but this is a more remote possibility. Further, there will be no migration of Chinese people to Russia.

China and Japan

Japan and China do not have friendly relations, mostly because of the past history. In1937, Japanese troops massacred an innocent Chinese civilian population of thousands. Though the Japanese government apologized to the Chinese government about its past, China did not consider it a true and meaningful gesture. Prime Minister Mr. Abe has taken steps to restore normal friendly relations between these two countries. Chinese and Japanese trade is booming. Before and during World War II, Japan was the most powerful country of Asia. After its defeat, Japan lost that position. However, Japan has the second largest economy in the world presently. China is coming up fast; they are the third largest economy and it is building military power. With the help of Russia, China may start challenging United States supremacy over time. Indeed, both Russia and China would like to gain the position of global superpower.

Japan and Germany once held these positions. China knows very well that going against Japan would be suicidal, as it would mean going against the United States. China may face a similar situation if it takes military action against Taiwan. Gradually, it seems friendly relations will be restored between Japan and China. Taiwan remains a troublesome area. If the Chinese government maintains its status quo position and does not attack Taiwan, then Japanese-Chinese relations will continue to grow closer and friendlier. It might take a long time for the Japanese and Chinese to consider themselves as equal partners socially.

China and Japan and a Possible Clash

China may very well come at par with the U.S. and Russia. As far as the economy goes, China has almost 2 trillion dollars in foreign direct investment. So in a decade, China will be matching the resources of the United States and will start playing the role of not only the regional player, but that of a superpower. China could become a source of threat to Japan and other countries. Prior to World War II and during that time, Japan was a similar power. The country had ruled over Korea and humiliated China during the war of 1937. Right now, Japan has a pacifist constitution written by the American forces in 1947, one that prohibits Japan from becoming a military power again.

However, over the next decade, if the Chinese government starts taking confrontational postures towards other regional countries in Southeast Asia, Japan might have to change its constitution. In such a case, the United States would also encourage Japan to start building a military force to match the Chinese threat. Presently, the United States is the only superpower that controls and dictates the global politics, but, in a decade, this might change with the rise of China. The United States will ultimately start looking for other Asian allies to counter the threat of China; Japan and India are two strong candidates suitable for such an alliance. It all depends how things move in the next ten years or so; if China continues to progress without confrontation then Japan will continue its assumed role of pacifist.

China and India

Since 1962, when China attacked India, the general public of India has become anti-China. The leaders of the two countries may say what they will, but the consensus is doubt and apprehension about one another, in the general public. These two emerging countries will be competing against each other, both short term and long term. India feels that China and Pakistan will collaborate to harm the Indian interests, which historically has proven to be the case. Since China is ahead of India in terms of economic and military power, it creates some problems for the Indian government.

Such scenarios prompt India to look towards the United States to protect its position. Similarly, the United States is likely interested in having an Asian ally to face the growing Chinese power. Since India and China are still poor countries in terms of GNI, these two countries will likely continue to live in peace for the immediate future.

It seems that India and China will follow independent policies consistent with their national interests and would not follow the guidance of American and Russian foreign policies. It is unfortunate that India has not done enough in restoring the Tibetan freedom cause, something that has occurred because it does not want an open war with China. The Western countries have shown their sympathies, but no practical and concrete actions have been taken, in spite of Dalai-Lamas best efforts. The modus operandi of foreign policies is based upon well defined self-interests and nothing else.

China and Southeast Asia

China is in a commanding position in Southeast Asia by all statistical measurements. China and South Korea are good trading partners; the volume of trade is increasing in both directions. Next to Korea, Singapore and Malaysia - both countries with a sizeable Chinese population - are set to increase their business partnership. Indonesia is trying to get Chinese investment along with other southeastern countries. Recently, China signed a free trade agreement with the Philippines, Thailand, and other southeastern nations. China carries a powerful influence over Vietnam, Laos, Cambodia and Burma. All of them are communist countries. China may consider these countries as buffer states. In the near future, the Chinese government may not follow an aggressive investment policy in these southeastern countries because it would like to spend money in places like Iran, Saudi Arabia, Nigeria and Russia to assure itself of adequate supply of oil and gas for its booming industry. It seems likely that Thailand will not be in the Chinese sphere of influence. The Philippines may also not get immediate attention. Trade relations between China and Taiwan are growing and will keep growing, unless war breaks out between these countries. Vietnam is trying to get investment from the United States and India too. In the long run, China will have a very powerful presence in most of Southeast Asia.

China and Africa

President Hu and Prime Minister Wen of China have made a number of visits to different African countries. China hosted a big friendship conference in 2006. More than thirty African country's presidents and prime ministers attended it. The Chinese government offered economic aid in addition to signing many developmental projects with these countries.

It is obvious that China is looking for oil and other natural resources for its booming economy. How China came out from the poverty level to become the third largest economy of the world within three decades is a matter of great interest for these African countries. Naturally, they would like to follow some of the Chinese industrial practices. After the death of Mao Zedong in 1976, Chairman Deng changed the fundamental industrial and political policies of China. "Wealth is Beautiful" is a policy that changed China. Countries like Nigeria, Sudan, and Angola have oil, so China is building progressive commercial relations with them.

China wants to sell its products to countries like South Africa, Egypt and other up and coming African countries. India does not have any presence commercially in Africa, with the exceptions of Nigeria and South Africa. There is a sizeable community of Indians in South Africa; thus, the Indian government will sooner or later attempt to establish good business relations with it. Brazil, South Africa and India are discussing the establishment of a free trade zone. China itself is interested in Brazil's natural resources as well as agricultural products like corn to produce ethanol. The United States does not want to see China in its backyard to promote communism. In the immediate future, China will continue to advance its trade and aid policies in Africa. There is no big competition from other countries; African countries will welcome Chinese business relations. Presently, China is not making any big moves in the Middle East socially, politically and economically.

CHAPTER 6

Global Influence of England

Time moves on and nothing is permanent in this world. History tells us how civilizations moved from one place to another and how nations have risen and fallen from glory. The rate of change now is fast, never seen by mankind before, and it is exploding exponentially. So what is going to happen to our world ten years from now is not an easy prediction to make.

Back in 70s, nobody was predicting that China would become one of the most powerful countries in the 21st century. We did not know that USSR would disintegrate into many countries in 1991, and that communism would no longer be a domineering force in world politics. How countries in Asia and elsewhere, including India, would change their destinies from socialism to open market economies, we could not project back in 90s. So the world has changed and is changing continuously. Let us look and make some more projections.

ENGLAND

Before World War II, England ruled over the world; the sun never set on its empire. However, the World War changed the destiny of England; it did not have the economic power to keep its former empire in tact after the War Country after country were granted freedom and the greatest power was reduced to a secondary position in the world stage. The lion that was England just vanished away. Even with its secondary position, England still has a large voice in shaping the global opinion. Military wise, it has a modern air force, efficient navy, and a powerful standing army. It is the main supplier of military armaments to many Asian and African countries that does include India and Pakistan. England is the birthplace of the Industrial Revolution; even today it has a huge industrial production base and is the leading manufacturer of many industrial products. England at this point in time is lagging behind the United States and Russia in terms of military strength, but is ahead of Russia in terms of Economic Power. England, along with the United States, is the most influential voice in the global political arena. England can never regain its former glorious past, but it will continue to dominate the events of global importance.

The Gross Domestic Product will continue to go up by 2% or so per annum in the coming decade. People will be better off in terms of wealth and have a higher standard of living. England may not completely embrace the European Union, but it may advance towards closer relations with it. The monarchy will continue to play its constitutional and social role. The defense industry and service industry will become major sources of foreign trade, especially with emerging Asian countries like India and others. Export of military aircrafts, helicopters, tanks, battle ships, aircraft carriers, etc. to Asian and African countries will increase. England will continue to attract students from India, Pakistan, China, and other developing countries in larger numbers. The quality of education and learning will go up and research and development in all scientific fields will likely increase. The population of England will move up from 60 million people to higher levels, maybe around 70 million. More Eastern Europeans will make England their home. There will be less immigration from Asia and Africa in the coming decade. However, the local Asian-British community will play important role in British politics and business growth.

The most important ally of Great Britain will be the United States of America. Whether there is Tory party or Liberal, the foreign policy of England will not change much in actuality. If people like Mr. Sarkozy, the present president of France, keep coming to power, then there are good chances that England and France may become closer than they are today. In Asia, India may become a very close friend and ally of Great Britain and the local British Indians will play an important role in this trend. Germany and England would move on to friendly relations. There are no imminent dangers of any trade clashes. However, political point of views may differ. England would continue to influence the directions of the global politics, in the coming decade. Arabic countries like Saudi Arabia, Jordan, Dubai and Kuwait would maintain excellent relations with United Kingdom. It still has a tremendous influence in the African continent. Next, we shall discuss the global influence of France and Germany.

FRANCE

Like England, France was once a great colonial empire. It has established its supremacy in many countries of the world, notably in Southeast Asia and continental Africa. France and England fought against each other to take control of the colonies. France has a large standing army along with modern air force and navy. Its economy is the third largest in Europe, falling behind Germany and England. France has the reputation for great culture. General De Gaulle was not very enthusiastic to merge the French culture with the Anglo-Saxon's way of life. In politics too, the French were not speaking with the same tenor and tone at many times in history. The French are very proud of their language, their culture, and other things in life.

Things have radically changed now; President Sarkozy has openly said that he admires some of the Anglo-Saxon's way of doing things, especially their work ethics. France has come much closer to the United States and England than it ever was before. Will things change after Sarkozy is gone? It is difficult to say.

How much influence France has on the world stage? Most probably, it will have a lot of leverage when the country moves along with Germany. In the recent past, these two countries have been following each other consistently in world affairs. With Germany's economic might and France's military's superiority, these two countries can become a formidable force of influence.

France has a large influence in Algeria, Lebanon, and other Middle Eastern countries, and in Africa. The French have lost their influence in Southeast Asia. Vietnam, Laos, and Cambodia do not have any French connection. France will continue to play a leading role in the European Union and its affairs, and since it has rejoined the NATO Command, it will be an important player in shaping the world events.

Can France stand alone and try to play dominant role in the world's political arena, without the support of Germany or England? It is difficult to answer; the chances are it will not succeed. France does not have that audience. It seems though, France is moving away from antagonizing England and the United States. It is good sign for more stability and cohesion in building a safer world.

France plays a very important role in the global events. The European Union is the brain child of France and Germany. These two countries are the driving forces behind European Union. This organization of European countries is moving strong in the direction of removing barriers of borders, business transactions, duties, monetary exchange, travel documentation, and many others. It has now twenty seven members and its global influence is increasing in terms of trade, economic and financial policies. France is a permanent member of the Security Council.

President Sarkozy is a dynamic leader; he wants to bring about many changes in the French society. Very recently, laws were enacted to raise the retirement age from sixty to sixty two years; the "Burqa"-the veil-has been outlawed in France and many more reforms are in the list. Sarkozy is trying to open up the French entrenched ways, politically, socially and economically. France carries a powerful voice in the international arena; it is a nuclear power, has economic clout to dictate terms and is a highly competitive supplier of military hardware. It means a lot to many Asian and African countries. Germany has lost this edge after World War II. Algeria, Tunisia, Morocco, Lebanon and many African countries have great French influence.

In the next ten years, France will continue to make further progress with a growth rate around 2 % in terms of GDP. It is expected that France will continue to transform the European Union into a very powerful entity. The present population of France is 60 million strong. The GNI is $43,000 per capita. There are about five million people of Arabic and African origin living in France-the largest population of Muslims in Europe

The relations between France and England are getting warmer under Sarkozy. France and Germany were close allies during President Chirac and Chancellor Schroeder. It looks like France will continue to build closer relations with Germany and England in the next decade.

France will extend its area of influence in Arabic countries like Algeria, Tunisia, Lebanon, and other former French colonies in the coming decade. It is a nuclear power and it will be in the forefront in supplying aircraft – both military and civilian, submarines, faster trains, nuclear power stations, helicopters, tanks, and all kinds of military equipment to the growing powers of Asia, Africa and

Latin America. France will try to build good business relations with Asian countries, especially India and China. We do not predict any dramatic changes in the foreign policy of France towards Asian countries

GERMANY

Germany is the largest economy of Europe. With 80 million people and a technologically advanced society, Germany will continue to have a dominant role in the European Affairs, both socially and politically. Since it is no longer a military power, its role in the global arena is not great. The trade relations with Asian countries are normal, but not dramatic. Because of the past history of world wars, German interaction with Asian countries, even after sixty years from the end of World War II, remains small and insignificant. However, German companies are putting their investments in Spain, Greece, Poland, Hungry and other Eastern European countries. The major trading partners are France, Holland and England.

Germany will become more prosperous country in the coming ten years. However, the population growth will be nominal. Presently its GNI is roughly $43,000 per capita and GDP will maintain about a 2% growth per annum. Cozy relations with England will take a long time, but Franco-German friendship will continue to grow. Relations with Russia will be normal and unchanging.

German companies will continue to revive and build industries in the previously communist East Germany. They will be interested in setting industries in countries like Poland, Bulgaria, Romania, Spain, Russia, and other emerging Eastern European countries. We do not see any big investment surge towards Asian and African countries in the near future. A solid section of military business-hardware and technology-has been erased for Germany because of the outcome of the World War II. That holds true for Japan, too. These two Super Powers of the twentieth century will play important roles in the world politics and would continue to dominate the global economy in the twenty first century. Next, let us examine the global influence of Russia.

RUSSIA

Russia is moving towards democracy, but it is a far cry compared to Western countries democratic principles and actions. It is not a dictatorship, but it is autocratic state and it is what we can call somewhat of a communist, yet capitalist country. It will take sometime before we could see some similarity between Western democracies and new Russia. President Putin of Russia once said: The Western style democracy does not suit us.

In the next ten years, Russia will move towards establishing a more democratic apparatus and mechanism in their government. It might prove true that Russia would never become a democratic state in the sense what the

Western world understands. They simply do not have any democratic history. Prior to communism, Czars ruled over Russia and there was no democratic institution in place.

Russia is a great military power and a nuclear superpower. Just for that very reason, it will have a tremendous influence in global politics. Economically, it is no match compared to any of Western nation, but it has a big say in the emerging countries of Asia and Middle East. Russian leaders would like to maintain friendly relations with the Western countries and America since it has a lot of ground to cover, especially economically, with these countries.

Sometimes arrogance, national pride, and nuclear power can twist the minds of the national leaders and that leads to chaos and destruction. The new Russia would like to keep up its sphere of influence with those countries which once were part of the Soviet empire. As far as Western European countries are concerned, Russia will not be able to exert any significant pressure on these countries, mainly because it lacks economical clout. Also, there is NATO to help insure the safety of these western nations.

The Russian leaders talk about bipolar and multilateral centers of influence in global politics, mainly because they think they are great military power and they can dictate terms to other countries. If the leaders of the western countries and those of Russia get berserk, it could bring disaster to the entire world. That means the leaders of western countries would have to move carefully when they are dealing with the Russian leadership. We do not see any melting pot of western countries and that of Russia in the next decade. They will continue to move unilaterally of one another. England, France, and Germany will continue to build business relations with Russia but, socially and culturally, there will be distances.

Russia and Major Asian Countries

There was a time when the USSR was a domineering force in Asia. Countries like China, India, Egypt, Indonesia, and others were following the footsteps of the Russian model of government. For almost two decades (1950-1970), India and China followed the socialist doctrine for running their countries. Because of the common bond of Socialism, these countries of Asia were close. Russia has since lost much of its power and influence in Asia. Looking at the present political conditions, China is far ahead of Russia economically and it will continue to move in that direction.

Things changed in 1991 when the USSR disintegrated. China has its own independent foreign policy; it does not toe the Russian line. India is trying to align itself more with the United States rather than with Russia. Egypt has completely forgotten Russia. Countries like Iran and Syria still maintain close relations with Russia. Saudi Arabia, Jordan, Iraq, Lebanon, Algeria, none of these countries maintains close ties with Russia. Even the communist country Vietnam wants to have better relations with the United States. The major reason is that Russia does not have the financial resources to invest in other countries.

The common bond of socialism has disappeared. Russia still has some good connections with North Korea, but, practically, it does not have any powerful influence because of its inability to help out financially the corrupt and inefficient North Korean government. Since the fall of communism, every country is looking for capitalistic way of running business. However, there are still some notable exceptions in South America such as Venezuela, Peru, Bolivia, and others. The Russian sphere of influence has diminished considerably after 1991 and it seems likely to stay in that position for some time to come, till the Russian economy shows some dramatic improvements.

Russia and Europe

All of the Eastern European countries that once were loyal supporters of the USSR are now aligned with Western powers. Poland, Hungary, Romania, Bulgaria, and former Yugoslavian countries have all disconnected the old ties of fraternity and closeness with the present republic of Russia. In fact, all of them are good friends of America and the European Union. Russia does not have any crucial influence on these countries. Russia has an edge now in terms of higher gas and oil prices. The countries of the European Union have to maintain friendly relations with Russia because of this bargaining chip. Western Europe needs Russian oil and gas. As time moves forward, Russia will start moving towards the status of a superpower because, in a decade or two, Russia will build a good reservoir of money from oil and gas. Since it already has the paraphernalia of massive nuclear missiles and bombs, it will again start playing important role in the world politics.

There is no European country that openly embraces Russia. Consequently, Russia will take some time to start building some solid bases of close relations with Western and Eastern Europe. Some Middle Eastern countries, like Iran, Syria, and Palestine, might establish closer relations with Russia once it can afford to provide financial support to the other countries. Russia itself will take time to democratize its government structure. It is not going to be easy. It seems likely that days of Russian dominance in world politics has gone for good. Russia has to do lot of home work in order to catch up the higher standards of western countries.

CHAPTER 7

The Muslim World

MUSLIM COUNTRIES IN THE MODERN WORLD

We have to look closely and examine the influence of the Muslim countries in context of the Twenty first century. After 9/11 tragedy, many people all over the world consider Islam as a religion which is incompatible socially, economically and politically, with the modern world. There are more than one billion Muslim people settled in more than seventy countries of the world spanning from Africa, Middle East, Central and South East Asia, Far East to Europe.

We have to ask: Is it the religion or some other factors that govern our life, that are igniting all these kinds of problems at this juncture. Muslim clerics say that Islam is a peaceful religion, a tolerant religion that respects other religions and it is only the misguided people who are now terrorizing the world with their merciless actions of killing innocent people all over the world-whether it is in Iraq, Pakistan, Afghanistan, Palestine or anywhere else. Suicide bombers, Taliban militants and Al Qaeda have become a dangerous force to the welfare of the humanity.

Muslim countries could be separated from each other by the way the people of those countries lead their daily life. There are Muslim countries like Turkey and Lebanon where modern way of life is prevalent and thriving and there are many other countries where strict Sharia's laws have to be practiced and obeyed as in Saudi Arabia, Sudan, Malaysia, Afghanistan and Nigeria.

After 9/11, a lot of things have changed. The world could be divided into two: the Muslim world and Non-Muslim countries. The Muslim world has assumed world wide attention. Looking from the perspective of global influence that these countries could exert, it is clear that non-Muslim countries have to work closely with the Muslim World to remove misunderstandings and misinterpretations. When we look statistically at the economic data, a picture emerges that point out a wide divide between Islamic countries and non-Muslim countries. If we opt out rich Arabic countries like the United Arab Emirates, we come across few moderately well off countries; the majority of them are poor. Let us look at some of these countries.

Pakistan

The most talked about country is Pakistan; a nuclear power and home to the Taliban and Al Qaeda. It is a place where most of the plots against the United States, England, India, and other Western countries are hatched. The government is not capable of controlling these militants group despite massive and substantial U.S. aid. Pakistan has a powerful military institution; it has a modern structure of education, health care, judiciary and other modern facilities. It is also a home of religious fanaticism-Koran Madarssas-Schools-where old century traditions are strictly followed.

Most of the Asian Countries have rampant corruption-degrees differ in each country. Pakistan could be counted as one of the most corrupt nation. With illiteracy in abundance, high unemployment and abject poverty when combined with eighteen century outlook towards the modern world, no wonder it has become a strong foothold of Jihad and Taliban. Right now, Western countries especially the United States is providing billions of dollars to reverse this course and stabilize the country before it is lost for good. It is no doubt that if Pakistan becomes another Afghanistan, it will become a big headache not only for the European countries but also for Asia. India would become a big target in such a scenario. A democratic Pakistan with non corrupt leadership and financial aid from financial institutions could become a progressive country in the long run.

United Arab Emirates

Kuwait, Qatar, Abu Dhabi and Dubai are part of the U.A.E. These cities and small size countries are flushed with oil and gas money. These countries are not anti-Western or anti-U.S. However, the money resides with the ruling elite families. There is no poverty, unlike other Middle Eastern countries.

The members of the ruling families have invested heavily in the U.S. and other Western countries. Because the general public is better off economically, there are no terrorist or Jihadist groups in these countries. This economic factor is a guiding indicator that points out that education, jobs, and modern teaching might solve the present day problem of terrorism which is raging in Afghanistan, Pakistan, and Iraq. The people living in most of the Middle Eastern countries are facing hardships because there are very few jobs; these countries are under developed and the leaders are autocratic. The common man does not know what to do except to listen to Mullaha's- Religious Pastors - narrow and short sighted version of religion. These people are generally ignorant of modern world. The poor and the illiterate person becomes a terrorist when he sees no door open to him except Jihad. This is unfortunate, but is a reality. Ten years from now, the U.A.E will continue to march towards Western way of living, and might change the course of direction of other Muslim countries by keeping its way of life.

Iraq and Afghanistan

These two countries will take many decades before their citizens will feel safe and ready to lead normal lives. The United States and Western countries are spending billions of dollars and providing military personnel to help the

Afghanistan government to fight Taliban, but what are the chances of success? The future looks bleak for Iraq and Afghanistan. Sunnis and Shiites in Iraq will continue to fight among themselves till Iraq is partitioned into two separate states. These two countries have taken a heavy toll on Western countries financially and in terms of human losses, especially the United States. Iraq will be remembered in history as a disaster for former President Bush's foreign policy.

Afghanistan's situation is equally bad. Taliban and Al Qaeda are not going away in the next ten years. There are good chances that they would become stronger than they are today and they will continue to harass the United States and its allies. NATO may not be able to fight wars in Afghanistan and Iraq because it is a different kind of war, similar to Vietnam's war. It will be difficult to predict the outcome of the present scenario that we see in these two countries. Afghanistan is a poor country and therefore it has its own problems, whereas Iraq has the religious divide problem of Sunnis and Shiites. It seems that the United States and its allies will give up one day and leave these countries on their own to decide their future.

Indonesia

The largest Muslim state in terms of population is Indonesia with its 230 million people. It is a moderate Islamic country and a developing country with a bright future ahead. President Suharto helped transform Indonesia into an emerging industrialized country from agricultural base. If the leaders of this country abandon the corruption practices that were present everywhere during President Suharto's regime, Indonesia could emerge out as a peaceful, industrialized, and modern Muslim country. If the economic conditions do not progress, the country may become a radical Islamist stronghold. Already there are some signs of anti-Western attitude and opinion. A few years ago, a militant Islamic group had blown up a hotel and restaurant in Bali, killing around 100 Australians. However, Indonesia is not like Iraq or Afghanistan. If we delve in history, Indonesia had a powerful influence of India in terms of social, cultural and religious way of life and even today Indonesia carries many similarities with Indian way of thinking. Indonesian names have Indian origin and Bali is a Hindu state. Hard headed Jihadists and religious extremists are frowned upon by the general public. We can say with good reasoning that Indonesia would never become a home of thriving terrorists and Islamists fanatics. Smaller groups of extremists and religious fanatics would crop up here and there, off and on.

Turkey

It is the only Muslim country that is rather free from terrorist, Jihadist, and fundamentalist organizations. Thanks to its founder Kamal Atrutuk, the country is secular and the people are not swayed by Sharia laws. The military sees that the government follows the principles of its founder. With a population of 75 million people and a GNI of around $7,000 per capita, Turkey is indeed a bridge between Muslim people and the West. It will be in the interest of Western countries to maintain close relations with Turkey because no other Muslim country offers a modern way of living. It is indeed a big transformation from the Ottoman Empire. It is unfortunate that Turkey does not have any strong influence over other Muslim countries. If we look at the Muslim countries of the world, we note that each country follows its own policies. Ten years from now, we hope Turkey would continue to follow secular policies and religious clerics do not dictate the policies of the government.

Malaysia

Malaysia became an independent country in 1957. It has a population of 25 million people with a GNI of $7,000 per capita. Sixty percent of the population is Muslim. It is a country where Sharia laws are being followed and the leaders promote Muslim culture. However, it is a moderate Muslim country, and militants and terrorists have not established their bases there as of yet. The Chinese citizens of Malaysia have helped the country to move towards the business culture and they are the richest section of the society. The government is run by Muslims; they have been taking a leading role in promoting the Muslim point of view and sometimes express anti-Western thoughts. At this time, Malaysia is close to Indonesia; they have similar languages and the same religion. It seems like that Muslims of Malaysia will not follow in the footsteps of Turkish people. It seems likely that they will be interested in leading other Muslim countries. Since Malaysia is not a poor country by Asian standards, extreme Islamists would not find it a breeding ground for Jihadi movement. It seems that elite Muslim class of Malaysia is inclined more towards Islamic way of life than perhaps a Pakistani or Lebanese rich class. That way, European values and cultural affinities would not be embraced by the Malaysian society, in general. It will lean towards Muslim way of life. However, extreme Islamic culture and way of life would not find favor with an average Malaysian. When we are talking about an average Malaysian, we are excluding Chinese and Indian community. We can predict with surety that Malaysia would not become a country of extreme religious bigotry and it would move with the western values of daily living-more or less, not hundred percent.

Saudi Arabia

It is a country which has 25% of the world's oil supply. The GNI is $12,000 per capita. It is the richest Muslim country. It is also a country of 18th century religious dogmas and antique way of life, especially for Muslim women. The society is miles away from the modern way of thinking. The country is run by an absolute monarchy. Saudi Arabia is the birth place of Prophet Mohammed, the founder of Islam. Presently, there are more than a billion people who are followers of Islam. Saudi Arabia has a powerful influence on other Muslim

countries, especially poor Asian and African countries. It is the birthplace of Al
Qaeda. Bin Laden is a member of the royal family of Saudi Arabia. All the
hijackers of 9/11 were citizens of Saudi Arabia and Egypt. It is interesting to
note that the monarchy of Saudi Arabia is not anti-west; in fact it is pro-America
and friendly to British interests. At the same time Saudi Arabia promotes Islam
in its strict format, to the rest of the world. Poor, uneducated and unemployed
Muslim youths in Pakistan, Afghanistan and other countries get financial
assistance in one form or the other from the Saudi Arabian religious institutions.

Algeria

Both Algeria and Tunisia have seen the terror of Islamist militants. The
fundamentalist Islamist organizations have established strong bases in these
countries. Just as with the Muslim Brotherhood organization of Egypt, these
Islamist organizations have a strong backing from the general public. People feel
that Sharia laws should be strictly followed and the Western way of life should
be discarded and condemned. Algeria has a good chance of overcoming the
influence of the fundamentalist groups because the middle class has a strong
influence of French culture and the Western way of thinking. If the country
could provide jobs for the masses, there is a strong possibility that it may follow
the path of secular Turkey. But if the common man remains poor and deprived,
the militant Islamist group would become stronger and popular. The same
analysis applies to Tunisia. It must be noted that Algeria and Tunisia are not hot
bed of terrorist organizations like Pakistan and Iraq. However, there is a large
group of people who believe in Sharia's rules and practices and discard modern
European ways of life.

Egypt

Egypt is the country where the Islamic Brotherhood organization originated. It is
an organization of Islamic fundamentalists, believer of strict Sharia's practices
and they completely disown European values and views, socially and politically.
President Sadat was gunned down in a parade by the members of this group.
Egyptian government headed by President Mubarak had been waging
continuous battle against Islamist Brotherhood Party. The common man and
woman of Egypt have overwhelming sympathy with this party. The reason is
that the general public is still very poor and the existing government has not
delivered the desired goals of elimination of poverty and raising the standard of
living for the common masses. The elite group of people is entrenched in
powerful positions. Inspite of massive American aid to Egypt, the country has
not made any sizeable progress. Unless and until the common man in the
country see something concrete to make his/her life better in the near future, the
long term future of Egypt looks dismal and dark. It is a shame that the
democracy exists only in name; there is no meaning to it in reality

Syria

It is interesting to note that in many Muslim countries, the head of state never gives up his position; he holds it for decades whether the public wants it or not. It has been true in case of Egypt, Syria, Indonesia, Malaysia, Iraq, Iran and Pakistan. Dictatorship and one man rule characterized these countries. President Assad of Syria was no exception. After his death, his son became the President of the country. Syria is the strong hold of Hamas-a revolutionary group of terrorists and a staunch opponent of Israel. The United States had branded Libya and Syria as terrorist states, at one point in time. Syria has a powerful say in the politics of Lebanon. However, we do not hear any news of Suicide bombers killing innocent people in their own country, though there is poverty and old traditional religious views among the masses

Jordan

The staunchest ally of the United States and the western countries in the Muslim world is the Kingdom of Jordan. The former King Hussain was married to an American lady who still lives in the United States. The United States has given lot of money to Jordan to counterbalance the anti-American voices raised in the Middle East. At present a vast majority of Palestinian refugee lives in Jordan. As such, Jordan has no big influence in the Muslim world but still it can be of big help to further the American interest. Jordan could become a shining democratic state as a showpiece to the Middle Eastern countries but the monarchy thinks that it is too early to follow the western model of democracy. Once a while, the Palestinian militants create trouble in Amman, the capital of Jordan to show solidarity to their brothers in Gaza and West Bank. But it is not a big deal and not a regular feature. As we see it now, Jordan would remain a good friend of the United States in the coming decades

LATEST DEVELOPMENTS IN THE MIDDLE EAST

The year 2011 has brought some very dramatic events in the Middle Eastern countries. It started with Tunisia. The younger generation of the country demolished the existing autocratic government and now it wants to establish a government for the people. Then, the same freedom movement spread to Egypt and President Mubarak had to go. Right now, the whole region is rising against autocratic rule and western style of democratic movement is spreading fast. A revolution is taking place. This new wave of freedom for democracy is spreading to Libya, Bahrain, Syria, Jordan and Saudi Arabia. We can call it a turning point in the history of Middle East and North Africa.

CHAPTER 8

Concluding Comments

We would like to conclude our analysis of the world's events with a positive note. Sixty five years have elapsed since we saw the end of the global warfare. During this time, there was no major conflict between the so called Super powers. In the first decade of the twenty first century, we witnessed the tragic 9/11; saw the bloody wars in Afghanistan and Iraq. In all these, United States was deeply involved. Luckily the opposite forces against the Americans were Iraqis, Al Qaeda, Taliban and suicide bombers from Pakistan- not Russians or Chinese.

If we round up the significant events, the spot light falls on Iraq, Afghanistan and then it moves on to, Iran, North Korea, Palestine and Pakistan. We shall once again look at the roles of World Powers and Super Power in our conclusion.

Let us scan the present Iraqi situation; where it is now and what the future looks like?

The big question that has to be asked is: Was the war in Iraq worth any dime? Most of the people in the world think "It was not". Millions of Iraqis have to flee from their country, billions of dollars went down the drain, thousands of innocent civilians perished and the end result is: though Saddam Husain is gone, the country is in the worse possible stage of chaos and political upheaval. It will take a long time for Iraq to come to a normal state-forget the progress part. The Iraqi war has put U.S.A in deep trouble.

There are very good chances of a civil war in Iraq. The democratic structure that is needed by the country is a distant dream. Iraqi people would never forget what they had to endure during this period of turmoil and hardship. The general public in Iraq could never look towards U.S.A as a country of "every body's dreams."

We feel Iraq would move slowly towards limited democracy. Americans in Iraq would not find it a place of security and friendly people. Suicide bombers would linger on for sometime and the general public would be skeptical of American values.

AFGHANISTAN

Afghanistan falls under the next glaring light. Eight years of war has produced no tangible results. The people have gone through hell-first when Russians were there and now when American and Europeans are trying to destroy Taliban and Al Qaeda. Abject poverty, illiteracy, nomadic culture and old fashioned ways of moving in life are solidly engrained in the society. Talibans Sharia's laws are repugnant and highly anti modern mode of living. Corruption is rampant throughout the established government circle. Drug lords rule most of the country side. Under these conditions, how the American and European countries could change the society. It is an uphill task. To change the culture, is not an easy task. It is unfortunate but true that Afghanistan is a country where lot of money, lot of education and tons of perseverance and determination is needed to turn the wheel of fortune. The alternative to leave the country in the hands of Taliban and Al Qaeda is too dangerous for the whole world.

President Karzai is not a charismatic leader; sectarian groups have powerful voice in shaping the structure of democratic set up-which is just not there. With the support from the western countries on a long journey, Afghanistan would be able to stand on its own feet with confidence and success. It will take a few decades. When the American forces move out, there could be a vacuum. A strong Afghan's leadership would be vital, at that point in time.

NORTH KOREA AND IRAN

A few months ago-May-June 2010-the North Korean army torpedoed a South Korean military ship killing number of soldiers. South Korea and U.S.A protested against the unprovoked action of the North Koreans .Subsequently, a joint military practice was organized by the South Korean Navy and the U.S to show the military strength of the two countries. Currently there is serious tension between the north and South Korea. The interesting part is that North Korea is still adamant and shows no sign of backing down.

We should remember that dictators want attention and they want to show to their country men that they are strong and they are not afraid of any other country. Like Iran, North Korea wants to become a nuclear power. North Korea and Iran are two arch enemies of the U.S and it looks like they could trigger off some kind of mini clashes against the western countries and the United States. North Korea could destabilize the South by such threats and provocation. Iran on the other hand-if it is attacked by the Israelis or any western power-could unleash a torrential powerful backlash from the Muslim countries.

It is a tough situation. The policy makers of the United States and the western countries have to walk the rope very carefully because the top leaders of both countries-North Korea and Iran- have complete control over their people and have supreme authority in their hands. History tells us that dictators are eccentric and they do not care for any logical reasoning for making their decisions.

There are good chances that these two countries could steal the thunder by provoking the United States and its allies into mini war. Mature countries like China and Russia would not take any chances to disturb the existing peaceful world environment. This reasoning does not hold true in case of Iran and North Korea. Things might change if the leadership in these two countries changes

At this juncture, North and South Korea could not be united in any kind of association-they are miles apart. In order to remove poverty in the North, the sitting leaders of the country have to compromise with the South Korean government. Arrogant leaders care for their prestige and power-they do not care what happens to the general public. Iran and North Korea have lost few decades of national progress by following the dictates of their present leaders.

A war could become imminent between Iran and Israel if the present leadership of Iran does not change its plans to become a nuclear power. It may also applies to North Korea .If North Korea keeps on nurturing its nuclear ambition , South Korea and the United States may finish off this dream.

China and Russia could play important role in reversing the present policies of North Korea and Iran. Russia and China have supported North Korea in the past and they do maintain good relations between them. Similarly, Russia and Iran had good relations in the past and they do have excellent communications in the present. Russia is helping Iran in setting up nuclear power generating plants.

Whereas U.S.A and western countries have voted for tough sanctions against Iran-for persuading its nuclear plans-Russia and China have opposed these sanctions. China wants Iranian oil for its industries and Russia wants to sell its military hardware to Iran. This is a solid reason for opposing sanctions against Iran. At the same token, we had seen that sanctions imposed against Saddam Hussain's regime did not produce any tangible results. What happened in the past may happen again. Israel might finish off the Iranian dreams of becoming a nuclear power.

We feel North Korea and Iran will recognize the gravity of situation. Weighing all the positive and negative aspects of the situation, it seems likely that both countries would terminate their nuclear programs and let the world breathe a fresh air of peaceful co- existence.

PAKISTAN, AL QAEDA AND TALIBAN

The present conditions of Pakistan are serious and in deep trouble. The economy is down, there is rampant corruption throughout the government and at the top of the situation, Jihadists, Suicide bombers and Talibanis are entrenching deeply in all parts of the country. Though billions of dollars are provided by U.S.A and other countries to help the Pakistan Government, it seems that the conditions would not improve soon. The present military chief Kayani may not stage a bloodless coup against the present government, yet the chances are that military might intervene if the situation does not improve and that would be the end of a democratic elected government. Only time would tell; it is difficult to predict what would happen in the near future

PALESTINE

The Palestinian question is difficult to solve unless the Israelis feel that they can live peacefully along with an independent state of Palestine. Right now, Israel is feeling the heat from the Iranian President who vows to destroy Israel once it acquires the nuclear bomb. In case Israel is forced to destroy the Iranians nuclear plants, there would be tremendous commotion in the Muslim world. Palestinian would be the first to raise hell against Israel and the United States.

SUPER POWER, WORLD POWERS AND CHANGING ALIGNMENTS

We see no big difficulties for the United States of America to retain the number one position in the world for at least two coming decades. It will be the only country to be called the Super Power-militarily and economically. With a flourishing and rising economy exceeding fifteen trillion dollars, there is no country in sight to match its mighty powers.

China would be number one runner up followed by England, Russia, India and France. Japan and Germany would be mega economical giants but they would not get into Super Power slot.

India could take second position bypassing England, France and Russia if its leaders chart out a bold and determined course of action. India has the potential to tie with China.

The present alignments between different nations would deviate a little but not much in the second decade of the twenty first century. The United States of America and England would retain a solid foundation of mutual trust and close cooperation.

India and Japan would move closer to the United States.

China would stand as a World Power edging towards a Super Power position.

Russia would be trailing in this global race.

Pakistan would likely to remain in good relations with the United States as well as with China.

India and Pakistan would not go together in the next decade. There are fewer possibilities of accommodation between India, China and Pakistan

Relations between India and England would move to a higher plateau

India, Japan and Australia might forge a deeper relationship in the coming decade.

Brazil might come up fast in this power race.

Germany would continue to be number one in Europe in terms of national economy.

The chances of North Korea and Iran to become nuclear powers are slim.

We do not see dark clouds of a major clash or a mini war shrouding our planet in the next decade. Getting rid of Al Qaeda and Taliban would not be easy.

The African continent would move slowly but surely towards economical progress.

The chances of a Global War in the next decade are slim; peace and prosperity would prevail

We see South Korea as a fast upcoming nation of global influence and a reliable friend of the United States.

European Union would embrace more countries of Europe; Turkey may not be able to join the Union because of the skepticism and differences in terms of governance and religion.

Germany and France would be the leading force in the European Union; England might not be in the forefront in encompassing its activities

United States may pay more attention to its own home ground policies rather than concentrate on Europe.

Latest Development India and China

Recently, year 2010, the Chinese Prime Minister Mr Wen made a goodwill visit to India. On his arrival, in New Delhi he said he has come to promote strong and friendly relations with India. China and India are not competitors; they are partners. He would establish good relations to boost business dealings between the two countries as well as establish better understanding of each other needs and aspirations. After the war in 1962 over border dispute, India and China never enjoyed warm feelings towards each other. After sixty years, things have started changing a little bit-but not much. Though the trade and business environment has changed considerably-the bilateral trade has reached sixty billion dollars-yet suspicion and feelings of non trust prevail among the common people of the two countries.

Prime Minister Dr.Man Mohan Singh of India reiterated that there is enough room in this world for India and China to coexist as friends and not as enemies or rivals. Mr Wen echoed the same sentiments.

At the end of visit, the joint communiqué mentioned that by year 2015, the trade between the two countries would hit one hundred billions. It was a very good sign. However, the major Sino-Indian problems remained at the same mark; no major break through was achieved. Chinese government did not support India on Kashmir, did not say any thing against Pakistan's support to anti-India terrorist groups, border disputes between the two countries remained intact, recognized the desire of getting a full membership of the Security Council for India but no open support was promised.

Indian government played its cards well. It did not recognize One China policy; in other words, it did not support the Chinese policy towards Taiwan and Tibet.

If we were to sum up the ramifications of this latest development, we can say that India and China would move along cautiously and they would continue to chart their own paths. Open war does not seem a possibility; competition between the two countries would prevail. It will be a long time when slogans like - Hindi Chini bhai bhai-Indians and Chinese are brothers-would be played over.

INDIA AND THE UNITED STATES

When Mr. Obama became the President of the United States, he was giving indications that he would establish very strong relations with China. His predecessor, President Bush was not very enthusiastic about building very close relations with China. Furthermore, Mr. Obama was sending signals that U.S.A might intervene in Kashmir. These two factors were very disturbing for the Indian government. Indian newspapers were predicting that Indian American relations would no longer be warm and cozy with the new president of the United States. President Bush was considered a very good supporter of India. But things started changing when Prime Minister Singh visited United States. Obama and Dr. Singh established close relationship and that changed the political road map for India. In the year 2010, President Obama paid a visit to India. This visit became a turning point. India and the United States were once again on the high road of better understanding and closer cooperation. Obama was welcomed in India with open arms. He and the first lady Michelle responded with grace and enthusiasm. United States supported Indian candidacy for the Security Council, condemned the actions of Pakistani terrorists groups and praised the Indian leadership in spreading democratic principles in running the governments. By this time, Obama had started realizing the importance of building better relations with India. The Chinese big picture had started fading-at least it had taken a more realistic place in terms of comparative outcomes.

United States of America has to find some leverage against the Russians and the growing influence of the Chinese. India and Japan are two natural choices.

Personal relations between the top leaders of the world carry a tremendous weight in formulating foreign policies. At this moment, India and the United States are moving in the same direction and the future for closer relations looks pretty good

FRANCE AND INDIA

The energetic President of France Mr. Sarkozy came to India in 2010 along with his wife Carla Bruni. This was his second visit to India. Last time when he had come as the chief guest of the government of India, he had written in the Taj Mahal visitor book" he will come back" True to his words he came back to see the Taj and at this time he was accompanied by his beautiful wife Carla. The couple was mesmerized by the beauty of the Taj-one of the seven wonders of the old world. Sarkozy has a different personality and has a more open vision of the world. He is friendly with the United States and with England. It is a big departure from the old policies of Mr. Chirac.

Sarkozy is more global in his outlook and realizes the importance of building friendly relations with the emerging Asian countries. India and China have taken important positions in his political map. Within a short span of two years or less, he has established good personal relations with the Prime Minister of India, Dr. Singh.

At the conclusion of his Indian visit, Sarkozy gave his full support for the permanent membership of the Security Council for India. He criticized the half hearted role of the Pakistan government by not curbing the anti-Indian militant groups which are openly supporting terrorism in India and other western countries.

The Government of India and France have signed business agreements to build nuclear plants in India. Sarkozy has indicated that he wants to establish closer relations with India. If this trend continues, we expect a warm welcome to Indians in France and with it a better business environment. But it will be a gradual process.

CHAPTER 9

Rise of Democracy

REVOLUTION IN MIDDLE EAST AND AFRICA

When President Bush made up his mind to invade Iraq, he elaborated his foreign policy by saying that America stands for democratic institutions and by dislodging Saddam Hussain, a banner will be raised which would start a new beginning for establishing democratic governments in the Middle East and other countries of Africa.

The Iraqi war was started in year 2003 and for the next five years or so, nothing changed in the Middle East. The Iraqi war did not help in establishing democratic governments in the Arab world. It is very true to say that outsiders can not impose democracy or any other kind of governing system unless the local people fight for it. When this happens, a revolution starts taking shape. And this momentous event happened in December 2010 in Tunisia.

SPARKS OF FREEDOM

This revolution of freedom began in Tunisia. A college graduate like many others in the country was very much frustrated because he could not get any job. He started selling vegetables and fruits on the street corner. He did not have any vendor license because he could not afford it. The local police beat him and took away what he had in his stall. This incident drove him to set himself on fire. The poor guy was left with no other choice but to take this action. He was severely burnt and after few weeks, he died. His death sparked a revolt among the young people of Tunisia. There were clashes and rioting against the police. This momentum of freedom forced the President to flee the country and take asylum in Saudi Arabia. The whole government was dissolved and the old autocratic rule was buried for ever. This movement for freedom was the resultant affect of existing poverty, high unemployment, lack of transparency in governance, rampant corruption, uneven distribution of wealth and autocratic rule. The younger generation of Tunisia rose against the ruling elite and established a system of real democracy; the voice of government for the people, by the people resonated on the streets of Tunisia.

DOMINO EFFECT

The bordering country of Algeria got the message from the freedom movement of Tunisia. Like in Tunisia, the younger generation started protest rallies against the established regime. The government of Algeria immediately took some pacifying steps to curb the revolt of the general public. It is a calm sea at this moment but it might bust in the near future. It is a matter of time. The chances are that the present regime would allow the common man on the street to share the national wealth on an equitable basis and make lot of changes in the present system so that unemployment, poverty, lack of equal opportunities and social disparity disappear soon. The other alternative would be a carbon copy of Tunisia. It has to be seen

EGYPTIAN DEMOCRACY

Going back to recent political settings in Egypt, we see a strong backing for Muslim Brotherhood organization from the poor and lower middle class Egyptians. President Saddat had kept the members of the organization away from participation in the government activities. Muslim Brotherhood organization believes in Sharias laws and encourages Egyptians to discard western culture and its values. President Saddat was assassinated by the members of this outfit. President Hosni Mobark followed the same policies towards Muslim Brotherhood. The members of the Muslim Brotherhood were barred from the election process and many of them were put in the jail. However, this organization was going stronger and it was challenging the elite of the ruling party. In the last Egyptian elections, members of the party alleged that it was a rigged election. President Mobark had been the President of Egypt for more than thirty years. He had run the government with an iron hand. The army generals and the business friends of the President had controlled the administration of the government during this time. This scenario was true till January 2011. Then, the mighty waves of freedom movement came from the shores of Tunisia. And things changed.

The democratic set up in Egypt was unable to provide the very basic needs of the general population. Poverty, high unemployment rates, second class educational institutions, lack of good health facilities, uneven distribution of wealth and non participation in the governing processes had become the highlights of the Egyptian democracy.

Egypt in the past had maintained excellent relations with the United States. Furthermore, Egypt has been receiving a generous amount of financial aid in lieu of this cooperation. Lately, some criticism had been forthcoming against President Mobark from the officials of the U.S government for not following the cardinal principles of true democracy.

In the wake of Tunisian uprising and revolt against the entrenched autocratic political leaders of the country, Egyptian people rose against President Mobark and forced him to resign and leave the country. It was a great victory for a genuine democracy

LIBERATION OF LIBYA

Colonel Gadhafi has been in power for more than twenty two years, in Libya. During this time, it has been a one man show; he ruled over the country with out any concept of democracy. Libya is rich in oil, so money is no problem. However, the general public is not getting the benefit of all this cash flow; only his family, his friends and faithful tribal leaders are cashing in. The average person is still poor; there are no good educational institutions and no political freedom. Like Saddam Hussain,Gadhafi is a dictator.

Things started changing in Tripoli too, after the democratic victories in Tunisia and Egypt. Rioting and public clashes against the government started erupting in different cities of the country. The rebel forces against Gadhafi took control of many industrial towns. A kind of civil war is now going on in the country; Gadhafi versus democratic group.

President Obama criticized openly, the Libyan ruler and asked him to get out.

At this point, the United States, England and France are taking the leading role to oust the Libyan leader from his throne. The NATO forces are bombarding the stronghold locations of colonel Gadhafi. Hundreds of people have died in the ongoing conflict and it seems like that it will not be an easy victory for pro democracy army. If the western countries keep up the pressure against Gadhafi, he is not going to last for a long time. The victory of democracy would prevail.

REFORMS IN SYRIA

Like other Middle Eastern countries, Syria has not made any sizeable improvements in terms of education, health, creation of jobs and political freedom. Just like in Egypt, the government has been in the hands of selected officials. The common man on the street has no voice against the ruling class. There is uneven distribution of national wealth. Most of the people are poor and yet they are toiling under the harsh conditions of non democratic structure.

President Bashar Assad has studied in England and is a medical professional; well versed in western culture and its values including democratic practices. Somehow, he did not try to incorporate those values that he saw in England and other western countries, in his own country. In its place, he decided to follow his fathers rules and regulations which were non democratic and autocratic in nature.

The rippling effects of Tunisia and Egypt are emerging in Syria, now. Troubles have started in Syria; people are raising banners of freedom and democracy. The police is hitting back and many people have been killed in this process. How far it is going to go depends upon the resolve and determination of the Syrian people. There are conflicting reports about pending reforms that would be incorporated by the government for setting up democratic structure in the country. President Assad knows very well that the strong wind of democracy that is blowing in the region would take its toll in Syria, too. Under these conditions it would be in his own interest that he establishes a popular, democratic form of government for the people, by the people

MONARCHY AND DEMOCRACY

Saudi Arabia

Monarchy and democracy can exist side by side without any problem provided a well defined structure is in place. England is a thriving democracy and it has a very popular queen. However, this is not the case in the Middle Eastern countries. Saudi Arabia has a well entrenched monarchy and almost no democratic structure. The king is completely autocratic; there are no ambiguities regarding his authority and power of command. There is no parliament of elected members. The king appoints his council of ministers and run the show. The word "democracy" is just not a popular word in this country. Under these conditions, can democracy thrive and flourish? The answer is not very encouraging.

All the turbulence of trouble and hope that is spreading like a wildfire in different countries of Middle East and Africa is not making any inroads in Saudi Arabia. The king is one of the richest persons in the world. He is giving away lot of money to his subjects and that is enough gratification. There is no ground for raising slogans of democracy and freedom of speech. It seems like that people are happy as they are and there is no reason to grumble and agitate.

Some voices were heard against the present regime but no body has the courage to openly defy the monarchy. Under these prevailing environments, there are no hopes for a democratically elected government and political reforms. The doors for democracy are closed for a long period of time.

Jordan

The political situation in Jordan is, little different from Saudi Arabia. There are traces of democratic structures. Though the king is in complete control and yet there is a parliament of elected representatives. There are some glaring differences between a complete democratic set up and a partially democratic institution. This scenario holds some validity in case of Jordan.

King Abdullah of Jordan acknowledges the advantages of a democratic set up but he says the country is not yet ready to embrace it. He may be right to some extent. However, given the present environment of freedom revolution in Tunisia and Egypt, the king must think about the consequence of not following a major shift in the political arena. Little changes may not satisfy a potentially dangerous situation of uprising against his rule. Chances are that the king would gradually move towards a more democratic set up in the country

Bahrain

Bahrain is a small island country, home of the 7th fleet, rich in oil and an ally of the United States. Unfortunately, the monarchy rules the country with an iron hand. The people are frustrated with high inflation, lack of good education facilities, selective participation in political and economical structure and very limited opportunities of employment. They want a democratic government, selected by the common man and not chosen by the king. The picture is not clear. Drastic reforms favoring democracy is the need of the hour.

UNSTABLE DEMOCRACIES

Pakistan

Presently, Year 2011, Pakistan has a democratically elected government. Three years ago, it was run by a military dictator, General Musharraf. Since its independence, Pakistan has gone through cycles of dictatorship and democratically elected governments. The United States and other western countries want to see democracy thrive in the country on a permanent basis. The problem is, whenever there is an elected government, corruption, crime rate, unemployment, inflation and self interest soars over the pole. This gives a good reason to well entrenched, powerful military junta to stage a coup and take over the reigns of the government.

Natural disasters, trouble with militants, Taliban and Al Qaeda have posed serious problems to the present government headed by President Asif Zardari, husband of Benazir Bhutto who was assassinated by the militants. With high unemployment, serious threats of violence, roaming suicide bombers, bad economic conditions and rampant corruption all over, how long would it take, for the government to crumble and fall apart? The United States is supplying billions of dollars to prop up the democratically elected government of Pakistan. If the conditions do not change for the better, there are good chances that the military would take over and that would be the end of the democracy.

Afghanistan

The United States and NATO forces have been fighting a war which is not easy to win. The military might is only one answer to solve the complex problems of Afghanistan. Very recently, elections were held to install democratically elected government in Kabul. Allegations of rigged election were voiced by the opposition leaders who were running against President Karzai. When we look at the prevailing conditions in the country, setting up democratic institutions need lot of resources. The country is not ready yet to comprehend its significance. Presence of abject poverty, few jobs opportunities, drugs, old ways of living, local lords, Sharia's Islamic laws and high illiterate population, is a far cry from a thriving democracy. Under these conditions, it is difficult to build structures of a modern democracy. It will take decades before we can say that Afghanistan is doing well in this area.

Selected Readings

Ardagh, John. *France in New Century*, Viking: London 1999

Bajpai, Kanti. "India and the United States Grand Strategic Partnership" *South Asian Survey:* January/June 2008.

Bender, David. *American Foreign Policy*, Greenhaven Press: 1972.

Breslin, Shaun *China and the Global Political Economy*, Palgrave Macmillan: 2007.

Chiozza, Giacomo. "A Crisis Like No Other? Anti-Americanism at the Time of the Iraq War," *European Journal of International Relations*: June 2009

Cohen, Laurent. *The Shape of the World to Come*, Columbia University Press, 2008.

Cohen, Stephen. "The New American Cold War," *The Nation*: June 2006.

Curtis, Lisa and James Phillips. *Revitalizing U.S efforts in Afghanistan*, The Heritage Foundation. October 2007.

Devereux, David. "The Sino-Indian War of 1962 in Anglo American Relations" *Journal of Contemporary History*: January 2009.

Franchetti, Mark. "New Cold War," *The Times:* August 2008

Ganguly, Sumit and S.Paul Kapur. *India, Pakistan and the Bomb*, Columbia University Press: 2010.

Gifford, Rob. *China Road: A Journey into the Future of a Rising Power,* Random House: 2008.

Goldstein, Joshua S. and Jon C. Pevehouse. *International Relations.* Longman: 2011.

Jacques, Martin. *When China Rules the World: The End of the Western World and the Birth of a New Global Order,* Penguin Press: 2009.

Kynge, James. *China Shakes the World: A Titan's Rise and Troubled Future -- and the Challenge for America.* Mariner Books, 2007.

Lees, Charles. *Party Politics in Germany*, Palgrave Macmillan: 2005

Lei, Zhao. "Trilateral Cooperation between China, Russia and India—Pleasant Achievements and a Broad Future," *China Report:* October/December 2008.

Maull, Hanns. *German Foreign Policy*, Palgrave Macmillan: 2005

Maguire, Lori. *The Foreign Political Discourse in the United Kingdom and the United States in the New World Order,* Cambridge Scholars Publishing: 2009.

Meredith, Robyn. *The Elephant and the Dragon,* W.W.Norton & Co.: 2007.

Milner, Susan and Nick Parsons. *Reinventing France,* Macmillan: 2004.

Reiedel, Bruce and Karl Inderfurth, *NATO commitment to Afghanistan's future*, Brookings Institution: 2007.

Remington, Thomas. *Politics in Russia*, Longman: London and New York, 2005.

Rogers, Paul. *Afghanistan state of siege*, Open Democracy.Net: July 2008

Sa'adah, Anne. *Germany's Second Chance*, :Harvard University Press: 1999.

Holmes, Stephen. *The State after Communism-New Russia*, Rowman and Littlefield: Maryland 2006.

Saich, Tony, *Governance and Politics of China*, Palgrave Macmillan: 2006

Salehyan, Idean and Marc R. Rosenblum. "International Relations, Domestic Politics, and Asylum Admissions in the United States," *Political Research Quarterly*: March 2008.

Shanker, Oded. *The Chinese Century* Wharton School Publishing: Philadelphia, 2004.

Stevens, Anne. *Government and Politics of France*, Palgrave Macmillan: 2003.

Thurston, Alex. *U.S withdrawal from Afghanistan,* Pub Agonist Press: March 2008.

Uberoi, Patricia. "India–China Initiatives in Multilateral Fora: Two Case Studies," *China Report*: July/September 2008

Vijaylakshmi, K. P. "American Worldview and Its Implications for India," *South Asian Survey:* September 2008.

Wall, Irwin. "France in the Cold War," *Journal of European Studies*: January 2008

Author's Biography

Ramesh Raizada is the President of R&R Business Associates—a Consulting firm. He has traveled extensively to different countries to collect and assess first hand information on global events and socio economical trends. Besides teaching, Ramesh is involved in projects related to national and international strategic policy planning, disarmament and conflict resolution.